MY NEW ENGLAND

. . . A WITTY TRIBUTE

Michael F. Bisceglia, Jr.

Amazon Press
2016

r.

DEDICATION

Some years ago, I met a woman who changed the course of my life. She took it in a direction I would never have imagined. She brought me back to New England.

In a nutshell, she is from Utah. I am from Massachusetts. We met while teaching in the same school in Las Vegas. The attraction was one blink less than immediate. She had never been to New England and wanted to see it. I was only too happy to show her. She immediately fell for it and wanted to move here. I, however, had reservations. I had lived all over the country, and did not relish the prospects of moving yet again.

I painted a very inaccurate picture of the place, based on the New England I had left some three decades earlier. There would be long winters with plenty of ice, driving problems, bitter cold and snow aplenty. There would be New England drivers, some of whom can be very creative. There was the fact that she wanted to set a course for the northeast, when most northeasterners of our generation were heading south. And, of course, she had to learn a new language . . . Bostonian. I also pointed out that she would be leaving her family behind. She, however, pointed out that I still had more family in the northeast than she could ever have imagined.

The woman would not be swayed. What else could I do? I returned. My wife had positive superlatives so say about everything! I was somewhat incredulous, but then I began to see everything through her eyes. I had left a wondrous locale in search of a better place, when, in fact, I was leaving the best place behind.

The locale, the myriad of cultures, the quaintness of small towns and the magic of the big cities, the grandeur of nature, the heartfelt earnest pride of true patriotism, the strength and endurance of so many families, the honest sense of true neighborliness and so much more all welcomed me back and made my wife feel as though she were truly a native daughter.

With her by my side, I thrill at every craft fair, every brisk autumn day, every wave that crashes on our shores, every victory notched by New England sports teams, every squirrel that races across our stonewalls, and every glass of wine savored on our front porch at sunset.

Thank you, dear lady, for returning me to my sanity. Thank you for having the wisdom to be part of a region where we can do much more than survive . . . we thrive. And, thank you for helping me to appreciate the majestic tapestry of New England. Without you, Janet, this book would never have been possible.

MY NEW ENGLAND

is an anthology of poems and articles pertaining to New England— its people, its history, its traditions and so much more.

Apart from the well-known actual people, events and locales, any names, characters, places and incidents are the products of the author's imagination.

Any resemblance to current events or living persons is entirely coincidental.

CONTENTS

ALSO BY MICHAEL F. BISCEGLIA, JR.

Gaelic and Garlic
Room 600
Border Storm
Morris the Flying Moose

Insatiable (Marc Siegel)
To Walk With My Brother (Evelyn Thornton)
Back To Good Health (Jack Daly)
*You Can Tell Your Kid Will
Grow Up to Be Librarian When . . .* (Richard Lee)

"What New England is, is a state of
mind, a place where dry humor and
perpetual disapointment blend to
produce an ironic pessimism that
folks from away find most
perplexing."

Willem Lange

"I don't hate it he thought, panting
in the cold air, the iron New England
dark; I don't. I don't! I don't hate it!
I don't hate it:"

William Faulkner, Absalom, Absalom!

"If you don't like the weather
in New England now, just wait
a few minutes."

Mark Twain

Book Cover designed and book published by:
DALY PUBLISHERS
PO Box 1584 Hampton NH 03843
603-601-2733   603-918-8973

TAKE ME TO NEW ENGLAND

Take me from this world and give me peace.
But while here, let me walk among the trees.
Let me feel the breeze before a storm.
On the coldest nights, give me fire to be warm.

Let me hear the white caps break upon the shore.
And smell the salt air when I open cottage door.
Let me see a line of geese cross the moon on high,
And northern lights aflicker in a winter sky.

Let my footsteps scrape softly on a bridge of wood,
And stand where brave men marched and stood.
Let me walk rock wall made entirely by hand.
And spy a distant farmhouse on rich and fertile land.

Let me walk a mountain ridge that fades into the haze.
Let me walk a thousand more all the mornings of my days.
And hear a mellow church bell ring in towns so far away.
And see the children run and play the games of yesterday.

Take me to a summer pond where dragonflies abound.
Where fish leap in a distant pool and make a single sound.
Let me hear a concert played upon a summer stage.
And read a book while breezes tempt to turn my page.

Let me listen to the radio as I did when I was young.
And give me fields of flowers that I may walk among.
Let me catch a snowflake as I did those many years ago.
Let me feel the wonder of the seasons as I live and as I grow.

Let me greet the friends I've had all these many years.
Let us laugh and talk awhile and hold each other dear.
Let me listen to my elders and learn from what they say.
Let me practice all the lessons learned from life's eternal day.

Let me sip from frosty waters so deep and, oh so pure,
Knowing sun-filled mornings with blessed avian overture.
Do take me by the hand. O, take me to the land
A land so rich, so good, so fair, O sweet New England.

Michael F. Bisceglia, Jr.

PLYMOUTH ROCK

There was a sea of mystery as to which rock
was the rock the Pilgrims scrambled over.

"Are we there yet?"

"Are we there yet?"

"If you two don't settle down, I'm going to have the captain turn this ship around and take us back to England."

"But Mom, Bobby always gets the porthole. I want to see the ocean for a while."

"Bobby, move over and let your sister see the ocean."

The year was 1620. A small band of people on a very small ship departed Holland after taking leave of England to find a place to practice their religion. Most folks imagine that John Alden jumped off the ship onto a large rock and said, "Priscilla, I'm home!" That's not quite true. You see, the Pilgrims couldn't land where they wanted. They settled for putting their feet down in the new world where Provincetown now stands. Sometime later, they found Plymouth Harbor and decided that the real estate was better there. Actually, there was no mention of a rock in any of the writings by the Pilgrims. The first reference to Plymouth Rock came about a century after the landing!

There was a sea of mystery as to which rock was the rock the Pilgrims scrambled over. In 1741, Elder Faunce had a wharf built over the rock his father claimed to be the one. Supposedly, his grandfather pointed that same rock out to him.

In 1774, residents decided that the rock represented the colonists' separation from England and decided to move it to a more prestigious location. Ever so gently, they lifted it from the ground. The rock, however, split in two. The folks who witnessed this saw it as a good thing. It definitely showed they were on the right path to split from England. The bottom of the rock was left where it had been found, while the huge upper portion was transported to the front of Plymouth's Pilgrim Hall.

A year later, British prisoners were captured from their ships in the harbor and made to walk upon the rock left in the harbor. The story goes that they were made to cheer the American cause. Yeah, right!

In 1835, an iron fence was built around the portion of the rock which had been moved. The bottom of the rock remained under the wharf where it had been left. The Pilgrim Society began to buy up buildings around the wharf with the purpose of preserving it.

In 1867, the two pieces of the rock were reunited in front of Pilgrim Hall. It was then that "1620" was cut into the rock.

In 1920, on the 300th anniversary of the founding of Plymouth Colony, the now-united rock was transported back to its original location. The old wharves had been removed, and the location had certainly been cleaned. It was at that time that the care of the rock was turned over to the Commonwealth of Massachusetts.

Over the years, some folks have taken home a little piece of history. The stone that exists today weighs about 10 tons. It is probably half the size of the original stone.

There are big doings shaping up for the 400th anniversary of the rock and for the Pilgrim Hall Museum. You'll definitely want to be alive to check out the festivities. Oh, in case you didn't know, the Pilgrim Hall Museum is the oldest continuously-operating museum in the United States. It just recently celebrated its 181st birthday.

Plymouth Rock rocks!

THE LAWS OF NEW ENGLAND

You will need to be well-versed in some of the laws.

I am a law-abiding individual. If a law exists, there has to be a good reason for it. I will assume, Gentle Reader, that you are of the same ilk as I (I know, don't assume). Thus, you will need to be well-versed in some of the laws (remember, I said "some") of this fair land of New England. Hang on, we're about to take a whirlwind legal trip through the region. Let us begin in Rhode Island.

It is an offense to throw pickle juice at a trolley. (You don't want to do that; it may stain someone's straw hat.)

No matter how much one begs, one may not be sold toothpaste and a toothbrush on a Sunday. (This must be written for the guy who ate the pickles.) Professional sports (except for ice polo and hockey) must obtain a license to play on Sunday. (One should have his toothpaste and brush before the game, too.) In Newport, it is illegal to smoke a pipe after sunset. (That settles it. I guess I won't be stargazing much in that town.) Now, on to Connecticut.

Under the law, a 16-year old boy could be put to death if he cursed at or disobeyed his parents. "Up against the wall, sonny; I told you not to use that Ipod." In Waterbury, it is illegal for a beautician to hum, whistle or sing while working on a customer. (Now, you know the reason why Ipods were invented.) It is illegal to clam at night. (I guess clams can't see you coming, and this gives an unfair advantage to the clammer.) In New Britain, it is illegal for fire truck to go over 25 m.p.h. when going to a fire. (If you live there, you better hope for a slow-moving fire.) In order for a pickle to be officially considered to be a pickle, it must bounce. (The law doesn't say that the object has to do this on its own or with assistance.) Let's move north.

In Massachusetts, it is illegal to drive Texan, Mexican or Indian (Native American . . . let's be politically correct here, huh?) cattle on a public road. (Keep those doggies rollin,' but not here.) It is illegal to take a lion to the movies. (Okay, but what if it's an MGM movie?) It's illegal to go to bed without having had a full bath. (Partial baths won't do?) Alcoholic drink specials are illegal. (Well, so much for fuzzy navel happy hours.) Children may smoke, but they may not buy cigarettes. (I suppose begging a butt is encouraged here.) Okay, a little northeastward now.

In New Hampshire, it is illegal to pay off a gambling debt with the clothes one is wearing. (I guess you can't lose the shirt on your back here.) One may not rake a beach. It is considered "maintaining a national forest without a permit." (I guess one doesn't need a building permit to erect a sand castle.)

One may not nod one's head, tap one's feet or, in any way, keep time to music in a tavern. (If you agree with this law, blink twice.) It is illegal to pick seaweed on the beach. (Certainly, if left unchecked, folks will be growing it in their cellars.) One may not run machinery on Sundays. (I suppose that means lawnmowers. Patriot fans must be excited about that one.) Now westward.

In Vermont, whistling underwater is illegal. (We don't want to scare the fish, do we?) Women must obtain written permission from their husbands to wear false teeth. (Does that keep 'em from whistling?) In Barre, all residents must bathe every Saturday night. "Okay, Fred, we didn't see you down at the community tub this weekend. Up against the wall and spread 'em." I, for one, will be glad to see this law stricken from the books. It used to be illegal to tie a giraffe to a telephone pole. (Let 'em get a cell phone like everyone else.) On to Maine.

After January 14th, a person will be fined for having Christmas decorations still up. "Put down that angel and step slowly away from the tree." Shoelaces must be tied when walking down the street. (Together?) One may not step out of a plane in flight. (Especially if one's shoelaces are not tied.) In Portland, one can't stroll down the street and play the fiddle. (Walking and chewing gum, however, is highly encouraged.) Also in Portland, it is illegal to tickle a woman's chin with a feather duster. (One might get life if one is playing the fiddle at the same time.)

Okay, you know the laws. Now, be careful out there.

THE SALEM WITCH TRIALS

. . . anything unexplainable was blamed on the girls.
Interestingly enough, the girls took the blame.

There are so many things that just say, "Gotta be New England!" Included on the short list are: fall foliage, Fenway Park, meandering stone walls, and, of course, witch trials. (No mother-in-law jokes, please.) Yes, we had them. In the late 1600's, Salem Massachusetts might have been considered "Witch Central." The place wasn't a coven deluxe, but it might have been considered the center of Puritanism in the region. The religious nature of the community possibly may have lent itself to a fear of the unknown. That fear, coupled with the desire to maintain the goodness of the flock, might have lent itself to some bizarre happenings.

Entertainment was extremely limited. Lighting quality was poor at best. The falls were cold and gray. Life was not to be enjoyed, but to be endured. Added to the mix, the French and Indian War was raging along the frontier; personal jealousies abounded; and anything strange was considered the work of the work of the Devil. After all, he was lurking around every "conah."

In February of 1692, there was some strangeness in the air of ol' Salem town. It seems a group of teenage girls (obviously in need of Ipods) formed a circle of friends. This group was considered to have too much time on its hands and was found in a collection of poses. (It sounds to me that they were merely caught playing "frozen tag.") From that point on, anything unexplainable was blamed on the girls. Interestingly enough, the girls took the blame.

"My Elizabeth has a cold. You gave it to her!"

"Yeah, I gave it to her. Waddaya goin' to do about it?"

Push came to shove and the girls were taken to court. (It wasn't really a court.) The preliminary hearings were held in a tavern. My guess is that the girls may have lost all of their teenage cockiness when they found out the charges were "like . . . serious."

One accusation against them was that they were seen flying about a room. (Sounds like more frozen tag to me.) Another accusation was that the Devil had struck them dumb.

"Okay, okay . . . when they talk to us, we just won't answer. They'll have to let us go."

"Hey, like great idea! Tick-a-lock. Throw away the key. This is great, huh?"

It that was their plan, it didn't go quite as expected. (Adults! Go figure.

Who can understand them?) From June through September of that year, 19 kids (14 of whom were girls) were publicly hanged for the crime of witchcraft. A male over the age of 80 was pressed to death by heavy stones. And, another four boys and girls (maybe as many as thirteen) died during imprisonment.

Salem hadn't cornered the market on witches completely. They were spotted in other New England states as well. Hampton, New Hampshire's Goody Cole preceded her Salem sisters by some fifty years!

One of the best ways to find out if an individual was a witch was to tie him or her to a log and then dunk them underwater for a period of time. If he or she came up alive, that person was a witch. If the poor person drowned, the individual was not a witch. Sounds fair, huh?

Salem has come a long way, and so has New England. The streets are better lit. There's plenty to do, and anything strange can be attributed to reality television. Reenactments of the trial can be seen periodically in the streets of Salem. It's great fun.

As I wrote this piece, I was thinking of my own teenage years. I let my hair grow, and I rocked to the music playing in my head . . . usually the Beatles or the Rolling Stones. My mom told me frequently that she couldn't communicate with me. I had changed!

Luckily for me, I didn't grow up on the streets of Salem . . . about 350 years earlier. I might not have grown up to be the tall, handsome, suave individual I am today!

THE BOSTON MARATHON

Initially, 18 guys took off when someone yelled, "Go!" That year marks the standardization of the 26 mile, 385 yard course.

In 400 B.C., the Greeks were taking on the Persians in a world-class, winner-take-all title match called the Persian Wars. It lasted a little over 40 years, so tailgating before and during the event was entirely possible. In 490 B.C., Darius took 25,000 Persians on an end sweep through the Plains of Marathon to Athens. Callimachus and Militiades appeared to have the wrong defense (maybe the original nickel defense) on the field; 8,000 men don't usually stack up well in that kind of brawl. Well, (here's the stuff dreams are made of) the Greeks stopped the drive for the end zone. No time left on the clock. Game over. Since ESPN didn't have a contract on the contest, somebody had to alert the media. Pheidippides got the job. He raced all the way to Athens; gave the headlines, and dropped dead. (My guess is he forgot to stretch before running.)

In 1896, the Boston Athletic Association thought it would be a marvelous idea to turn that informative trot into a race. Hence, the Boston Marathon was born. Initially, 18 guys took off when someone yelled, "Go!" (They didn't use a starter's pistol back then, and folks didn't start running from Hopkington until 1924). That year marks the standardization of the 26-mile, 385-yard course. In the early years, runners stumbled along over dusty roads to the finish line. (I'm sure there were more than just a few stubbed toes from unyielding New England rocks poking up in the road.) Over the years, the starting line changed from one site to another, and so did the finish line.

Initially, the race was held on St. Patrick's Day (probably a bad choice in Boston). In short order, it was changed to Patriot's Day.

Despite the road hazards (which included a closed bridge in 1907), the race continued to grow in popularity. That year, 124 runners entered the race. The numbers have increased slightly since then. Currently, over 20,000 participants test themselves against what is termed the world's second most prestigious marathon after the Olympic event. It takes over a half hour for the last of the participants to cross the starting line!

The Kenyans have dominated recent races, but there was another time. From 1922 to 1930, Clarence DeMar of Massachusetts won the event six times. The Bay State also produced another winner. From 1975 to 1980, Bill Rodgers won the race four times.

On a cold, windy day in 1970, Eugene Roberts of Baltimore, a double amputee, was the first wheelchair athlete to compete. He used a hospital wheelchair and completed the course in just over seven hours. To date, more than 1,000 individuals with disabilities have competed.

The race isn't without its characters (no event in New England would be complete without characters). John Kelley won it twice; he continued to run in the event into his 80's! Tarzan Brown (no kidding) won it in 1938, and topped off the event by taking a dip in a local lake. In 1980, Rosie Ruiz "won" the race. Sadly, she just happened to miss nearly all of the checkpoints along the route. She did turn up at the finish line to claim the laurel wreath. She was later proven to be unworthy of the prize.

A few years ago, two malcontents thought they could destroy a wonderful institution, the Boston Marathon, with a couple of bombs. They killed several people and severely wounded many others. The story didn't end there. Before the smoke lifted from Boylston Street, those on hand, New Englanders and visitors alike, jumped into action to help save lives. Those folks are to be commended . . . and the Boston Marathon lives on!

On a personal note, my brother, David, completed the event twice. His test time was a non-award winning 4:44:44. It didn't matter to anyone. He had beaten the course, and he was a proud member of the Rosie Ruiz Track Club of Worcester.

THE FLAG OF NEW ENGLAND – THE SYMBOL OF LOVE

For several years, it was a banner in progress.

Okay ladies and gents, you're going to have to bear with me a moment here. I'm going to attempt to make the biggest connection since the Great Cable connected Europe to the United States. Ready? Here we go.

We all generally know that Valentine's Day is generally symbolic of love. Yes, yes, there are traditional ways for one to show said 'love' on this day. Flowers - colorful but short-lived. Chocolates – delicious but fattening. Diamond rings – expensive but then again . . . very expensive. There are other gifts suitable for the occasion that would certainly be appropriate to place in the hands of the one who is loved by another. Stay with me now; we're making a giant leap here.

Alright, the year was 1775. In June of that year, the British attempted to regain control of the city of Boston by encircling it with cannons and commanding the area from the heights. Sounds simple enough, but the British ran into stiff opposition from the colonists. The British far outnumbered the Continental forces by over two to one odds. They had superior fire power and were better disciplined; they may have made two strategic blunders. First, they landed their forces too far away from their objective, and had forces too thin to completely encircle and cut off their enemy. The colonists took advantage of abandoned buildings to fire on the red-coated British. The colonists, running out of ammunition, eventually hurled rocks from rooftops at the red-coated foes. All the while, the Flag of New England flew bravely atop the breastwork at Breed's Hill, the rallying point for rebel forces. Still with me? Good.

Now, what is the Flag of New England? For several years, it was a banner in progress. In the 1620's colonists chose to honor the Penacooks who helped them to survive their initial winter by placing the pine tree, the Tree of Great Peace, in the top left hand corner. In 1629, the colonists added the shield of St. George's Cross to the same corner. In the mid 1700's, a field of red was placed around the cross; it very much resembled the British ensign. That same decade, the field of red was replaced by blue to make a firm distinction between New and Old England. There you have it, a flag under which New Englanders fought to secure their freedom from England. So far, so good? Okay, then.

In the early days of the second millennium, Child Bride visited scenic New

England with the love of her life. She absolutely fell head over heels with the region. There is no historic marker to do justice to this event. Suffice to say, the couple moved lock, stock and VCR to scenic southern New Hampshire from the southwest desert. NOW, here comes the big connection.

Knowing that Child Bride loves New England with an unbridled passion, I thought, "What better gift can I give the one I love than the flag representative of the region she now espouses?" Yes, truly, the Flag of New England is the perfect Valentine's Day gift.

Now, that's what I believed. The reality is that a box of chocolates might have made a better choice.

LAKES OF NEW ENGLAND

*The lakes of the wondrous realm of the northeast are gener-
ally surrounded by truly spectacular scenery, and are nestled
among some of the prettiest mountains on the planet.*

No one has lakes like New England has lakes. (Okay, so Minnesota has one
or two, so what?) We have them large. We have them small. We have them
round, and we have them long. No matter where you live in the greatest region in the country, you're not far from one, or two, or ten of them.

Yes, New Yorkers will tell you they have one or two large bodies of water.
They may even claim Ontario and Erie as their pride and joy. We all know
that size isn't everything. Besides, the Pin Stripers can claim ownership of
only part of those lakes!

You may ask, "Well, what makes New England lakes so darn wonderful?" The answer is "They're simply magnificent." You can't ask for better.
The lakes of the wondrous realm of the northeast are generally surrounded
by truly spectacular scenery and are nestled among some of the prettiest
mountains on the planet.

Let's start with some of the names. What great names! New Hampshire
has Lake Winnipesauke. It appears on hundreds of different post cards
and has a history going back over hundreds of years. Translated from Native American, it means "Smile of the Great Spirit." And, speaking of great
names, try LakeChargoggagoggmanchauggagoggchaubunagungamaugg! It
is found in southern Worcester County in Massachusetts, and it means, "You
fish on your side of the lake. I'll fish on my side of the lake, and no one fishes
in the middle." It also goes under the name of Webster Lake. Lake Sunapee,
which means "Wild Goose Lake" in Algonquin, is located in western New
Hampshire and contains three lighthouses. Talk about picturesque!

Whether the lakes bear names denoting their place in Native American
heritage or not, they are beautiful. Many lakes of the region are hundreds of
feet deep and are homes for some tremendous lunkers. Nearly every lake has
a fish or two, the sources for some of the greatest New England fishing stories
ever told. The "ones that got away" are still lurking out there, just waiting to
take your bait, snap your pole, and provide you with the fodder for a great
tale.

I know, I know. You don't fish. That's okay, too. If you use a paddle, an oar,
or a camera, you will still love the lakes of New England. There is probably
nothing more thrilling, more stimulating or more relaxing than an excursion

around the lake of your choice in a rowboat, canoe, kayak or sailboat. Throw in a few white caps, and you'll have an adventure saga to rival that of Treasure Island. Snap a couple of shots of the grandkids or grandkids (or the wife), and you'll capture some great moments you'll want to treasure.

Unlike lakes in so many regions of the country, our bodies of water are generally not man-made and are bigger than a bread box. On trips across the country, I have been disappointed over and over again when I heard of a "great lake." The claim was usually followed by, "You gotta go there." I am embarrassed to say that I have driven hundreds of miles to those puddles with nothing around them of wondrous scenic beauty as is the case in New England. Adding mayhem to melee, I usually had to pay an admission fee to get my toes wet!

Winter, spring, summer or fall, a New England lake is a jewel to enjoy. But let's keep that our secret, shall we?

FREEDOM TRAIL

Boston is where the American Revolution began.

Q.What did Mrs. Revere say to her son?

A. Paul, do you want to go for a ride?

Yes, I know. . . a very bad joke. This, however, is not a joke. Boston is where the American Revolution began. That is a concept that I find difficult to grasp. I live on the outskirts of a city that gave birth to a nation.

Imagine the personalities! Today, we think it is a huge deal to bump into an aging rock star in a pharmacy; or meet someone who vaguely resembles a long dead star, or chat with a guy who knows a guy who knows a guy . . . In the late 1770's you could drop into Revere's for some dinnerware, catch Washington at the dentist, Hancock might be buying some writing supplies and Franklin may have been walking in the Commons with a new ball of string. (Yes, I know they didn't all live in Boston. Maybe they just happened to be in the city for the weekend to enjoy a cup of tea.) In any event, this area must have been simply hopping some 200+ years ago!

A person can catch a glimpse of the way things were so many years ago if she or he cares to meander along the Freedom Trail. It is only fair to warn the perspective walker, things are not as they were during Colonial times. That would have been next to impossible as metropolitan Boston matured through the centuries. Someone strolling the Trail can take in a number of sites along some cobblestone streets, but it is a journey well-worth taking.

I'm not going to bore you, gentle reader, with all of the intricacies of how the Freedom Trail became a reality. Suffice to say, journalist William Schofield had the idea for it in 1951. In 1958, the basic plan was laid out. Between 1964-1984, there was more planning; incorporation became a reality; some restoration was accomplished and lots of fund-raising had to be done. (It took longer to prepare the Freedom Trail than to actually fight the Revolution!)

Just think of some of the items that can be seen in the short span of a walk: the site of the Boston Massacre, the U.S.S. Constitution, the Old North Church, Faneuil Hall, and twelve other sites of no less importance. The walker (or trolley car user) will definitely have a full day becoming acquainted (or reacquainted) with the birthplace of this nation's heritage.

Try this out for size . . . let your imagination take over as you walk. Do you see the carriages and tri-cornered hats of folks on the street? Can you see a line of Red Coats marching down Beacon street? Is Old Ironsides running out her guns? Who are all of those men meeting in that tavern? Are there one or two candles shining in that church tower?

Bring the camera and wear some good comfortable walking shoes. Enjoy a truly American experience. Tours include costumed actors who present all pertinent information in a easy-to-understand manner . . . all the better for me to understand.

CANDLEPIN BOWLING – THE ULTIMATE TEST OF ENDURANCE

Beginning in Worcester, Massachusetts in 1880, candlepin bowling has tested the physical ability (not so much) and frustration level of generations of individuals who seek something semi-athletic and semi-social.

Football? For wimps. Hockey? Nothing to it. Soccer? Rugby? Mountain climbing? Fagetaboutit! Candlepin bowling . . . now, there's the ultimate test of endurance. Nowhere else but in the great Northeast (okay, there are a few hundred places in eastern Canada . . . and one real trooper in Cincinnati, Ohio) can it be found.

Beginning in Worcester, Massachusetts in 1880, candlepin bowling has tested the physical ability (not so much) and frustration level (oh yeah, and then some) of generations of individuals who seek something semi-athletic and semi-social. (It is a great first date location for you women who want to hear what a prospective husband might say should he attempt to hammer a nail and miss.)

Now, how difficult can the game be? Looks easy enough – ten pins, a little less than 16 inches tall, set in a standard bowling triangle, to be knocked down by balls, about the size of the type used in croquet, weighing less than three pounds. There are ten frames with three shots to a frame. The pins, dead wood, which are knocked down (if any) stay down. The bowler gets to use (or avoid) them to attempt to cream the pins still standing.

Speed doesn't really matter. Most bowlers roll something faster than a Tim Wakefield knuckleballs, and less than a supersonic Curt Schilling fastball. Accuracy is everything. Hitting the head pin (that character in front of all the others) and part of the other two directly behind it, is most desirable. Theoretically, the collision between the ball and pins should create an explosion sending pins into one another which would leave nothing standing. That's the theory. The reality is that pins seem to exercise extreme courtesy in their attempts to try to avoid one another.

Is the game popular? You bet. New Englanders will shovel out from a blinding nor'easter; drive ten miles through winds and deepening snows, and trudge the length of a football field through hip-deep whiteness to meet their teammates for league competition.

And, if someone from Bangor to Bristol has a fever of 105 or so to accompany his or her two broken legs, he or she can always catch the pros whipping that little orb down the alleys on TV. Nothing cures the flu faster than seeing a guy who should hit those little critters – miss! "Ah, I could have made that shot." (Cough) "What a choke." (Wheeze) "What are ya aimin' at?" The next alley?" (sneeze) "I made that shot three times last week." (Honk)

I took Child Bride (former desert rat from Las Vegas and a woman who has been recognized for hitting a 265 in ten pin bowling) to the home of the true sport, a candlepin bowlerdrome, as part of her "get acquainted tour" of the region.

"This looks like fun," she cooed.

She missed the first half dozen shots.

"Cursed things (not really an actual quote.)"

She missed the next dozen shots.

"Gimme a stupid (not an actual quote) ball!"

She hit the end pin for a score of 1. There was a big smile followed by total composure.

She was hooked.

Michael F. Bisceglia, Jr.

THE SECRET OF NEW ENGLAND CLAM CHOWDER

*What made it especially tasty was
the use of the secret ingredient.*

Discretion is the better part of valor, and New Englanders can be very discrete, especially when it comes to revealing the secret of the best clam chowder in the world. Yes, I said it. No idle boast. Best clam chowder in the world!

The word "chowder" (correctly pronounced chow-dah, if you live in the most fabulous region of the United States) is a curious one. The best guess is that it came from the French word for caldron. Certainly, a chaudiere sounds like a properly austere item in which to brew up a batch of this mouth-watering cuisine. Amelia Simmons's American Cookery (1800), the first American cookbook, gave the first recipe for chowder. The recipe called for bass, salt pork, crackers and other items, but clams were nowhere to be had. By 1836, clam chowder was well known in Boston and beginning to find its way across the country. Originally, it was thought that it was another way for sailors to enjoy fish. (What's not to enjoy?) Anyway, by the end of the century, other items were being tossed into the pot (or chaudiere, if you're so inclined), including lots of cream and butter. What made it especially tasty was the use of the secret ingredient. Is your mouth watering yet?

At some point in the 1830's, Rhode Islanders tossed tomatoes into the mix, but New Englanders, purists that we are, began associating this strain with New York, and referred to it as "that terrible pink mixture." They couldn't have despised it much more if it had pinstripes. This bastardized brew was labeled Manhattan Clam Chowder. All right, enough about New York!

The Great Chowder Debate raged into the 20th century, and reached a flash point when Mary Alice Cook published Traditional Portuguese Recipes from Provincetown. She claimed that her family used tomatoes in chowder when she was a girl. Portuguese or worldwide? Hmmm. Interestingly, in 1939, a Maine legislator introduced a bill to make it illegal to add tomatoes to the pot. There was, however, no argument about the use of the secret ingredient.

Clam chowder became a staple in New England, and the use of salt pork or bacon was used consistently. The argument about the "best" chowder was one of constant debate. Amounts of ingredients were always subject to scrutiny. Strangely, no argument occurred when potatoes were tossed into the pot in the 1880's. This fete was attributed to Maria Paola from Danbury, Connecticut.

By the mid 1900's, folks up and down the East Coast, as far south as Maryland, were tossing just about everything into chowder including all sorts of vegetables and chicken! (A bird in clam chowder? Oh, please!) Today, most folks will agree that there really is no such item as traditional New England clam chowder (except that tomatoes are frowned upon). It is the concoction that takes the edge off of a raw afternoon or a dish to be savored after shoveling out from a wicked nor'easter. It is a New England family tradition to hand down from one generation to the next great family recipe, including the use of that special ingredient.

And now . . . that special ingredient . . . On second thought, nah, you just might go and tell a New Yorker!

NORMAN ROCKWELL

No words are spoken in Rockwell's masterpieces. None have to be. We know the words. We know the emotions. We know those expressions. They are ours. They are us.

It is my humble opinion that no one epitomizes the wonderful qualities of New Englanders as does Norman Rockwell. Certainly, his art was not solely scenes of life in this fair region, but he just seemed to capture the memories, true or imagined, that most all of us seem to hold dear. The subjects were not necessarily of landmark events, although surely he depicted several of those; the activities of everyday life are what I found to be the most engaging.

The scene of the little "runaway" boy sitting next to a policeman enjoying an ice cream in a soda shop; "Surprise," depicting a classroom filled with love for a teacher; the "Dr." and the Doll," in which a kindly old physician takes a moment to assure a young girl that her doll is in good health; and one that has always touched me deeply, "Breaking Home Ties," in which a world-weary father is sitting on the running board of the family truck with the anxious son, who is waiting for the bus and about to leave home surely touches the heart.

No words are spoken in Rockwell's masterpieces. None have to be. We know the words. We know the emotions. We know those expressions. They are ours. They are us.

Rockwell has born in 1894 in New York City (I guess we can forgive him for that little oversight). He always wanted to be an artist, so he dropped out of school to enter the New York School of Art at age 14. He was commissioned to do Christmas cards at sixteen. From then on, the world was clamoring for his works. In his teens, he became the art director for Boys' Life, and later he did the official cover for the Boy Scout Handbook. Later, his artwork graced the covers of the Saturday Evening Post.

Rockwell just seemed to focus on those aspects of human nature which touch our purest selves. There was nothing devious or cynical about his characters. They were simply humans being human at their best. The boys racing away from a forbidden beach in "No Swimming;" the sailor adding his newest love's name to his arm in "The Tattooist;" or the grandfather being searched for a present by a young lad in "The Gift," bring a collective lump to our throats. All of Rockwell's paintings seem so familiar . . . they very well could be snapshots of life, past, and present, in New England.

And, who can forget Santa Claus on all of those Coca-Cola advertisements? I believe that his image of the jolly fat man is the one most Americans conjure up when they start hearing all of those nostalgic songs played during the holiday season.

The artist didn't always focus on the general theme of nostalgia for his paintings. The poignant "Do Unto Others;" the stirring "Freedom of Speech;" and the awe-inspiring "The Four Freedoms;" just touch our feelings of patriotism and what America should be. "The Problem We All Live With" simply chills us with stark reality.

Rockwell's Vermont years spanned 1911 to 1978. The Norman Rockwell Museum is located in Rutland, Vermont. The Norman Rockwell Studio and Museum is located in Stockbridge, Massachusetts. I guess it safe to say that New England was as taken by the man, as the man was taken by New England. For a real treat, you'll want to make arrangements to attend the annual reenactment of Norman Rockwell's Main Street at Christmas in Stockbridge, Massachusetts. Call the local Chamber of Commerce. Find a pet sitter for the cat (do take the kids), and go! You'll thank me for it. And . . . you're welcome.

DON'T SKI NEW ENGLAND – IT'S ADDICTIVE!

Seriously, one will not find Alpine peaks or the Grand Tetons in New England. The Appalachian Mountains are a little older, and therefore, a little gentler than those other ranges.

Consider yourself warned. Skiing New England can be most addictive. Don't say you were never told. Okay, now for the details.

New England is a relatively small chunk of territory. It's one-third the size of Texas and three times as beautiful. (Okay, I'm biased. I admit it.) Inside that region, skiers have their choice of sixty-six sites. Sixty-six! You can practically leave one and be in the parking lot of another.

The obvious question is "Which one is the best?" The answer is, "I'm not going to tell you." You have to make that choice. Many of these resorts have everything the average (or above-average) skier wants . . . and then some.

Let's establish one thing right here and now. I'm not a skier. I've never been on a pair of skis in my life. And, for the record, I don't snowboard either. I am, however, a proud New Englander. And, like most proud folk from this wondrous region of winter white, I've been to ski resorts (primarily to enjoy the fireplaces in the lodges . . . which happen to be near the bars . . . which happen to stock great single malt scotches . . . which I happen to enjoy about every day of the week with the letter "a" in it."

But, does New England have any great skiers? Hmm, oh yeah. Try this list for size: Steve Ouellete, New Boston, NH; Chris Johnston, Cape Neddick, ME; Bill Bethel, VT; Tom McCollum and Larry Voekler, Pittsfield, MA; Rod Aller, Lakeville, CT; Rosanne Puleo, Boston, MA; Wendy Hill, Rutland, VT; Gay Folland, Conway, NH; Lisa Desnmore, Hanover, NH, and, last but certainly not least is gold medalist, Bode Miller, Easton, NH.

Seriously, one will not find Alpine peaks or the Grand Tetons in New England. The Appalachian Mountains are a little older, and therefore, a little gentler than those other ranges. One will find good skiing, decent-sized mountains, and miles of smiles to cover all of one's shushing needs. As a matter of fact, the common denominator among those who ski the Northeast is the ear-to-ear grins of our blade runners. I have numbers of friends and relatives who ski New England. They're hooked. They have great stories to tell, and they look as though they stepped out of the pages of any ski magazine. They're lovin' it.

And why not? Great locale. Terrific skiing. Magnificent vistas. Good food and grog. Super nightlife. Did I leave anything out? Nope. I didn't think so.

There is a downside to motoring through the moguls along the Mohawk. Sooner or later the snow will melt . . . work will beckon . . . and you'll be down to your last pair of underwear. In other words, all good things must come to an end. Well, yes and no. It always manages to snow in New England, and there always seems to be skiing aplenty . . . some great lodges . . . with some great fireplaces .

THE MANSIONS OF NEWPORT

*The mansions of Newport, along the rugged granite cliffs
of the Atlantic Ocean, represent a time when America had
some folks with some very big bucks.*

The following piece should be read with the throat thrust out slightly, the mouth slightly agape, eyelids partially lowered, and with an insufferably arrogant attitude. Feels uncomfortable, doesn't it? Oh well, it's only for a few hundred words.)

Child Bride loves New England. She also loves the Home and Garden Television Network. (Yes, I realize there's a slight stretch there. But, to my wife's way of thinking, the connection is as rational as peanut butter and jelly.) As part of our "Get Acquainted Tour" (in my case, re-acquainted), Child Bride just had to "take in" (her term, not mine) the mansions of Newport, Rhode Island. I practiced my haughty laugh, rolling headshake, and Roosevelt-like speech accomplished by not moving my jaws. I was ready.

The mansions of Newport, along the rugged granite cliffs of the Atlantic Ocean, represent a time when America had some folks with some very big bucks. It came at the turn of the twentieth century. The Industrial Age was in full swing, and New England had more than its share of factories and mills. Those places made more than shoes and wire; they also made money! The gentry with the money wanted to be away from the factories (but not too far away) and live in a place of beauty. So, they headed for the coast.

For the record, when the Titanic went down, so did the bulk of America's aristocracy. Their mansions remain, and the tour is spectacular. Entry is free at many of the estates; some charge a small fee for entrance. A visitor may walk; take a bus; ride a horse-drawn carriage; ride a bike; or (my personal favorite) charter a Rolls Royce (chauffeur optional) for the occasion.

I'm not going to provide details on all of the mansions. Suffice to say, they're an eyeful. Do allow me to give just a tad of information on one of them . . . The Breakers (note the capital "T" in "The"). The place has 70 rooms! That's a lot of weekend dusting. It was built in 1895 in Italian Renaissance architecture. It was owned by Cornelius Vanderbilt II. He just happened to be the bigwig at the New York Central Railroad. The Breakers is elegant . . . breathtaking, actually. Vanderbilt loved big parties. Having 200 guests or so was no big deal. (Too bad he's not around to hose a Super Bowl shindig.) My two favorite items are: bathtubs with hot and cold fresh and salt water, and a child's playhouse large enough to accommodate a family of four . . . and their dog!

It's so breathtaking, in fact, I had to go sit down on one of the 40 steps to catch my breath. That's the spot where all of the help at the mansions used to hand out to gossip about their bosses. Juicy conversations? You bet.

You'll love The Breakers . . . and The Chateau sur Mer . . . and The King-cote. By the way, does your house have a name? Mine does . . . The Money Pit. (Note the capital "T" in "The.") Did I mention that I'm painting the cellar?

Okay, relax your face and lose the attitude. The article is finished.

NEW ENGLANDERS
AND PATRIOTISM

*The birth of this great nation happened right
here in proud and noble New England.*

New Englanders may or may not be any more patriotic than any other region of the country, but it certainly does seem that way. Let's examine the history of this claim. That tea didn't end up in the drink by itself! Paul Revere didn't go for a midnight canter in Savannah, and that "shot heard 'round the world" wasn't fired in Flatbush!

Call it destiny. Call it what you may, but many of the circumstances which occurred to bring about the birth of this great nation happened right here in proud and noble New England. Those of us from the Great Northeast tend to bear the responsibility of that tradition proudly.

States which bear mottos such as: "Live Free or Die," "Freedom and Unity," "By the Sword, She Seeks Peace Under Unity," "I direct," "He Who Transplanted, Sustains," and simply, "Hope" send a message to its inhabitants and to the rest of the country . . . "America is worth the effort, and we make that effort with valor."

Monuments to fallen heroes since the onset of America to the present dot the landscape proudly and in abundance. Public squares, streets, parks, buildings, and more bear the names of men and women who have paid the ultimate price to keep America alive and safe. New Englanders choose to remember, and remember proudly, those from the region for what they did for us and the nation.

The Red, White and Blue greet the morning sun and catch the twilight glow from thousands of flagpoles on homes and in front yards throughout the region. Route 1, from the Canadian border to the doorway of New York is festooned with Old Glory to state boldly to anyone across the Atlantic, "This is America . . . land of the free and home of the brave!"

Veterans' Day, Memorial Day, the Fourth of July, and the like are not just days off from school or occasions for firework displays in the region. They are a call to remember and a reminder of what a terrific region and remarkable country we have. As little leaguers, Boy or Girl Scout contingents, American Legion or VFW posts march in parades, little tykes through seniors wave miniature flags and doff their hats to honor this fine country. As miniature those flags may be, there is nothing miniature about the true spirit of love that the folks here share for all that is right and just about America.

The reverence and decorum shown by all during the Pledge of Allegiance in school assemblies is expected of our children, and our children respond in kind. The torch is definitely being passed proudly to the next generation.

The continuum of the essence of American spirit from the first settlers to the most recent immigrants is a bond to New Englanders. We remember the past. We acknowledge the present. We live for the future. We want our children and grandchildren to understand and appreciate the greatness of the region, and from it, the greatness of America.

Yes, New Englanders are patriotic, and for good reason. The tree of America has its roots firmly planted in our rich and rocky New England soil!

THE FISHER CAT

This character has a very luxurious dark fur coat
and could be mistaken for a house cat.

Maine has the Coon Cat, but New Hampshire has the fisher cat. You need to know right up front that this critter is not a cat; not a fisher; and certainly not a pet. A fisher cat is a carnivore, and it has a voracious appetite.

This character has a very luxurious dark fur coat and could be mistaken for a house cat. It measures up to thirty inches in length, and has a bounding gate. It could be found in a tree or in the tall grass by a river or stream. It has dark, penetrating eyes and, for all the world, appears as harmless as a hamster. Don't be fooled.

It weighs up to twelve pounds and has five extremely sharp, retractable claws on each foot . . . all the better for tearing meat away from bone, my dear. Its diet includes everything from mice to porcupines. They're close cousins to the wolverine and they're great hunters. They have been known to store food from kills or other carrion while they go about seeking an additional food source.

Child Bride and I were trying to track down anything antique that would fit in our back seat as we drove through the southern New Hampshire countryside on a snowy Saturday morning. As we turned a corner, Mr. Fisher Cat bounded through some exposed reeds by a stonewall and stood up.

"I don't know what it is," I said to my beloved, "but I'm going to try to get it to come to the car."

I stopped and gently opened the door.

"Ahhh, I'm not sure that's the best idea you've ever had," she said as the critter brought itself up to its full height.

"Oh, everything's going to be fine. Maybe I can get close enough to touch it."

"You might want to get back inside," she said. She enunciated each word slowly and clearly.

"I'll be just fi-"

At that moment, the mysterious critter glared directly at me and flashed a mouthful of long, nasty-looking teeth. I'm not in way a psychic, but I'm certain it was saying, "Take one more step, my ignorant friend, and I'll have your hand for dinner."

One can, however, shake hands with a fisher cat. In fact, one could spend a whole afternoon with a number of them and have a terrific time doing so. The Fisher Cats, an affiliate of the Toronto Blue Jays, is the semi-pro team in Manchester, New Hampshire. Take my advice, buy some peanuts and crackerjacks, and enjoy the ball game. For added fun, take a long-distance photo of that critter in the woods ... a very long-distance photo.

Recently, a fisher cat set up shop on our back deck. It was midnight. The howls were otherworldly. That critter definitely wanted my lasagna leftovers. I didn't oblige him. I went to bed ... but I did close and lock the bedroom door first!

Michael F. Bisceglia, Jr.

THE NOTCHES OF NEW ENGLAND

These notches are one of the aspects of New England which set it apart from so many regions in the United States.

About 15,000 years ago, long before I was born, the glacier retreated northward from New England. Its impact on the landscape was little more than slightly dramatic. The ice had been here for some thousands of years, and as the temperatures rose, dramatic changes took place in the countryside. One of the most startling effects was the fact that this rocky region was literally carved or gouged into new shapes. These long tears in the landscape are called notches. That is a very pleasant term for some very distinctive terrain. These notches are one of the aspects of New England which sets it apart from so many regions in the United States.

The land has had a chance to mellow in the last several millennia, and what we have now are simply awesome delights. Beautiful coldwater streams flow through so many of these notches, and the mountains, which stand sentry to them offer some great skiing and marvellous trails for hiking. Franconia Notch, located about midway through New Hampshire is a fine example of the majestic terrain left behind by the glacier. Just to give you a snapshot of how powerful the glacier was, in the middle of Franconia Notch is a boulder over 80 feet in length, nearly 40 feet in width, and 20 feet high. It was simply left behind as one might cast off a pebble from a shoe.

If you're an outdoor person at all (truthfully, if you don't care for the gifts which Mother Nature bestowed on New England, you're in the wrong place), you'll love taking a canoe ride along some of the picturesque rivers flowing from these notches. If you have a yen for the more frosty things to do, you might try ice climbing the sides of some of the frozen faces of the mountains. When you're in the region, you'll be travelling along the Kancamangus Highway. On the roadsides, you'll be seeing signs for the Old Man of the Mountain. Don't worry if you can't find him . . . he left.

Smugglers' Notch in Vermont gets it name form the activities which occurred there around 1807. President Jefferson banned trade with Great Britain and Canada. Great idea at the time, but it didn't do much to help those folks living in northern New England. So, taking matters into their own hands, they developed their own little trade route toward Montreal. Cattle, whiskey and other goods all found their way to the north country through this small gap in the terrain.

Today, you'll be hard-pressed to find Canadian cattle moving down the slopes, but you will find some places to camp and some beautiful lodges for ski enthusiasts. If you're a fall leaf peeper, you probably won't find a more suitable locale than here to do your peeping.

Pinkam Notch in Maine is simply an ideal place to go for a stroll. The white birches of Pine Mountain (Yes, I know, "Why not White Birch Mountain?" I dunno.) are truly a spectacle. Nearby is the Ravine Trail through the Alpine Gardens. If you are a wild flower connoisseur, you won't want to miss a trek there.

The Ice Age glacier made its way across the northeast and effected the six New England states. The three northern states: Maine, New Hampshire and Vermont appear to have had the most dramatic alteration. The southern states: Massachusetts, Connecticut and Rhode Island, although affected, may attribute at least some of their wonder to Volcanic activity from 200 million years ago.

Okay, are you ready to go 'notching?' Let's see . . . hiking shoes, water battle, walking stick and snacks. Perfect, right? Wrong! You forgot your camera. Make sure you have plenty of batteries for your digital camera. You're going to need them. All right, now, get along with you. Scat!

NEW ENGLAND CEMETERIES

Sea captains, accused witches, patriots, slaves and
British soldiers are resting beneath its soil.

Why are New England cemeteries surrounded by stonewalls or iron fences? The answer is that people are dying to get in. Okay, bad joke. The truth is, New England does have many cemeteries. After all, we have a heritage that goes back to 1620. I'm not advocating packing the kids in the car and trundling off to the one closest to you; I am saying that some of the very old cemeteries in the region are worth your time if you care to visit. They're fascinating.

I won't say it happens with every walk in the woods, but quite frequently someone will trip over a rock in an overgrown area only to find it is a long-forgotten cemetery. Many of these areas hold only a few dozen graves. In some cases in New England, cemeteries have been found when construction crews began a new project. Along Route 1, just outside of Portsmouth, New Hampshire, graves in a very small cemetery are found only a few feet from the curb.

Older cemeteries were not necessarily in a prominent location in the urban centers of the time. Burial sites for slaves were haphazard, at best. Many were located behind the local churches. In more rural areas, lineage may be traced through the position of headstones in family plots on the clan's homesteads. Often, the granite headstones will do much more than delineate the names and dates of birth and death of the deceased. They may indicate what caused the individual's death and possibly include a short epitaph of or by that individual.

Call it my grave sense of humor, but I do enjoy a chuckle at the wit carved into some of these stones. Here's one from Enosburg, Vermont:

Anna Hepewell –
"Here lies the body of our Anna
Done to death by a banana.
It wasn't the fruit that laid her low
But the skin of the thing that made her go!"

Here's another from Hatfield, Massachusetts:

Arabella Young – 1771 –

"Here lies as silent clay
Miss Arabella Young.
Who on the 21st of May
Began to hold her tongue."

A wanderer among the old headstones may wish to take along some butcher paper and a few charcoal pencils to make a few rubbings of some of the more intriguing stones ... and there are many intriguing stones! Remember, New England has a very colorful history. Sea captains, accused witches, patriots, slaves and British soldiers are resting beneath its soil. Some folks, however, don't want to be recognized ... even in death. Such is the case of someone from Stowe, Vermont:

I was somebody.
Who, is no business
Of yours.

So there!

CAMPS

Camps are where New England families go, and grow,
reunite and remember. Camps are where friendships deepen.

New Englanders cope with winter. They shovel. They salt the sidewalks. They hang storm windows, and they toss on the long johns for three of four (or five) months. They do all this and more with the hope that a warmer remainder of the year is just around the corner. And, even before the last icicle has fallen from the north eave, many New Englanders make the trek to their place of serenity . . . their camps.

A camp, to a resident of the Great Kingdom of the Northeast, is not like Camp Winnebago where your parents may have shuttled you off to learn of bees and butterflies. When a New Englander goes to his camp, he's going to a nostalgic location that creates wonderfully warm memories to last through a lifetime of nor'easters.

Camps may be found by ponds, lakes or streams. They be located near the Atlantic shore or at the base of a mountain. They are the retreats most people search their lifetimes to find. They may have front porches, or not. The blueberry bushes might grow just outside the window or in the next meadow. A raccoon may live in that hole in the attic or down by that big pine tree where Marge and Joe carved their initials only twenty-seven years ago.

Camps are where New England families go, and grow, reunite and remember. Camps are where friendships deepen. The marshmallow fire always seems to be blazing. The fireflies are more numerous than the stars, and Uncle Charlie is always hysterical.

Nothing is ever perfect in a camp. It's supposed to be that way. After all, it's a work in progress. Somebody's always tapping a nail into a loose shingle or putting another two-by-four down as a back step. The raft could use a new chain, but there's always next year. And, the "N" in routed wooden sign that should read "MY BLUE HEAVEN" has been gnawed away by beavers. Those things will get done. They always do. But things just seem to move in slow motion at a summer camp in hazy New England.

There is something totally calming about those camping times. They are sensual delights. Food always tastes better. Leaves blowing in the wind sound more soothing. And, the colors of the forest critters seem sharper. And, one more thing . . . the sleeps are always deeper.

My friend's father had an old Air Stream that he anchored near a small pond in rural Spencer, Massachusetts. A radio somewhere in the place played music from the '40's, and the smell of bacon frying always seemed to hang in the air. I don't know what it was about that little place, but the moment I would toss a line in the water just off the back porch, I had to take a nap.

My Uncle Tommy had a camp near a lake in Gardner. It was a place where the entire clan would gather throughout the summers . . . lots of laughs . . . lots of hot dogs . . . lots of sunburns . . . and lots of memories. The hours seemed to last only minutes, and the days went by all too quickly.

If you happen to be talking to a New Englander during an ice storm and he suddenly seems to grow particularly quiet, he's not having some sort of attack. He's fine. He'll be back in the moment. He just did a cannonball into the lake near the trees. He didn't bother to dry off as he hustled up to the picnic table for a glass of lemonade and a hot dog slathered in mustard. He can hear Tommy Dorsey playing somewhere off in the distance . . . and he smiles.

QUALITY OF LIFE
SHOWS THROUGH

Best place for peace of mind: New England – You can walk down a country road a thousand times and see something to cause the corners of your mouth to curl upward each time .

I will not get into a debate with anyone as to which survey using which set of criteria surveying what grouping of people determines the "best state" in country. If I did that, I would invite more flak than filled the skies over England in WWII. I'll make this easy. I've taken a look at a number of polls (I don't want to mention names here. I'm trying to stay politically correct by remaining apolitical.) in my attempt to crown the best state.

Numerous factors were considered, all of which are valid. Some of these include: safety, education, senior care, road conditions, cost of living and employment. As safely as I can put it, New England is at least better than half of the states in the country. Did I hear screaming? No? Good. My determination of this region may be slightly biased. After all, it is a six-state region as well as being a nation unto itself . . . Red Sox Nation. I'm not going to mention which state topped all honors. That's gong to be your homework assignment. I'll give you one clue . . . it has the shortest shoreline in America.

I think the factors for consideration are just a little narrow. My personal determiners are much less rigid. Here's my personal box score non-statistical chart:

Best place for peace of mind: New England – You can walk down a country road a thousand times and see something to cause the corners of your mouth to curl upward each time . . . the first buds of spring . . . the sun coming out after a summer shower . . the aroma of ripe apples on a fall breeze . . . a calico cat dishing under a fence in winter are just a few of my personal favorites.

Best place to play a game of cribbage on a front porch during a summer shower: New England. Add a couple of Adirondack chairs and a glass of lemonade, and you're one step shy of heaven.

Best place to strengthen the bonds between generations by holding hands wading in the Atlantic surf or strolling along a lake: New England. This is best done with a grandchild holding both grandparents' hands. Best place to have treasured friends for a lifetime: New England. Start early, and grow the connection a little more each day. Share a movie, a snowball fight, an ice cream sundae, a double date, a wedding, a baptism and, yes, gray hair.

Best place to mature: New England. It's impossible to just age here or collect dust growing old here. There's so much to do . . . so much to see . . . so much to do better and to teach to someone else. From friends of libraries to church group volunteers to blood donors, those of us who are blessed enough to live in New England find that we thrive by doing. We don't just pass the time; we make time to do so much!

Best place to enjoy a scenic drive through six states . . . to ponder the majesty of the ocean . . . to muse at the expanse of a great lake . . . to wave at another country . . . and to wink at folks in pinstripes . . . all in one weekend: It has to be New England. It's not just a region. It's a nation . . . Red Sox Nation!

SCRIMSHAW
THE ART OF THE SEAS

Many of the great whaling ships of the 1800's were built in
Bath, Maine, and the home port for the whalers was
New Bedford, Massachusetts.

Say the word "whaling" today, and you might just start a brawl. Politics aside, the fact remains that whaling and New England are very much tied together. Many of the great whaling ships of the 1800's were built in Bath, Maine, and the home port for the whalers was New Bedford, Massachusetts. (No punches thrown yet . . . that's a good sign.)

Many of the sailors on whaling ships grew up in the trade. Most started as cabin boys and worked their way toward being full-fledged sailors on board these sea-going factories. The boys learned all of the skills necessary to be accomplished seamen. One of the true skills that all the men had to learn was how to deal with long periods of boredom between chores and actual activities of whaling. One of the skills was the production of fine scrimshaw pieces.

Essentially, scrimshaw is the art of carving from pieces of ivory or bone. For the sailors on board the whaling ships, whittling on an antler was virtually out of the question. Their medium was the bones and teeth of whales. (Sorry, there'll be no segment on this topic on HGTV.)

I find a few elements of this ancient craft to be particularly amazing. (My amazement . . . not necessarily yours) First of all, these artists were whalers . . . rough, hearty men who lived by their wits and skills to survive the perils of the sea. Second, they produced their art on board dimly lit ships on a rolling ocean. I have to take my hat off to them, these sailor artists, to sit with a very sharp object in hand while attempting to make fine cuts in a resistant bone while swaying to the beat of the ocean is probably a little more than I could handle. Ever!

These sailors took a bone in one hand and a blade in the other and carved everything from a smoking pipe (complete with fine figures carved into the bowl) to toys for kids back home. They etched out scenes of whaling adventures, historical scenes, beautiful women, kitchen tools, jewelery boxes, sewing and knitting needles, knife and sword hilts, toothpicks, and the list goes on and on.

Pieces of the actual ships were fashioned from the bones of the seas as well.

Not only were these bones fashioned to be functional pieces such as belaying pins, they were fashioned artistically. It is necessary to keep in mind that these fellows worked with simple knife blades. They didn't have the electric and electronic computerized gadgetry that exists today to enhance this process. Yet, these sailors carved some truly tremendous and awe-inspiring pieces.

There are several places where the public can view individual pieces of scrimshaw in New England. More often than not, what is required is a lot of curiosity and good luck if you happen to be prowling the coastal region of the great northeast. If you don't want to wear out that much shoe leather, you might amble down to the Whaling Museum in New Bedford. It's well worth your time to visit the Age of Sail, and to especially take in the art from that era.

THOSE BEACH TRIPS
OF YESTERYEAR

Ah, those wonderful beach trips of yesteryear.
Who can forget them?

Those of us in the gray hair set remember a time in the not-too-distant past when travel around New England wasn't done with the ease in which it is accomplished today. Not by a long shot. An hour-long trip today was a trek.

Growing up in Worcester and traveling to Hampton, New Hampshire required as much preparation as the Allies planning the invasion of Normandy. We never knew what was out there and we simply had to be ready.

"Blankets."

"Check."

"Flashlight."

"Check."

"Stocked cooler."

"Check."

After the necessary items were stored in the car, it was checked out from stem to stern. Tires, oil, water, gas, extra belts, battery . . . everything got the once over. We didn't want to break down out there in no man's land. So, we had to make sure we had enough provisions to keep us alive for a day or so.

Next, we had to plan our trip so as not to encounter traffic. This was virtually impossible since this was shortly after the dinosaurs left and just before the interstates were built. We were going to go through every village, town and hamlet. There was no telling what mishaps could occur in those towns.

"Okay, so we'll leave about five so we won't run into the early morning traffic around Shrewsbury."

"Well, the night shift will be getting off from work around Framingham."

"So, we better leave about four-fifteen."

"But we'll run into the truckers hitting the diners before we get to Boston."

"Right . . . right . . . and there'll be all that traffic from up north heading down to the Cape."

"You bet and don't forget all that construction along the way."

"Oh, yeah, get the kids. We gotta leave right now!"

Upon arrival, four or five hours later, the unpacking ceremony began. Everything was lugged into whatever quarters were rented. An hour later, three-fourths of what was packed was toted off to the beach. It is no wonder why the adults promptly fell asleep as soon as the towels were laid out.

"Hey Dad, wanna play catch?"

"Uh, not right now, son. My shoulders are hurting me from driving."

"Okay, mom?"

"Don't wake your mother. She's exhausted from getting ready for this vacation."

The most amazing thing would happen five minutes later. All of the people you left behind in your neighborhood would be sprawled out under their beach umbrellas right next to you. All of the thousand kids you left behind and hoped to lie to about your trip to the beach were spending the week in a rented cottage right next door!

The week would pass all too quickly. The check lists were again brought out and the trip home was underway. What I found interesting was listening to my folks later. The conversation didn't center around sun and surf. It was what route we were taking next year and how much better time we could make if we didn't pack this, that or the other thing.

Ah, those wonderful beach trips of yesteryear. Who can forget them?

DUNKIN' DONUTS
. . . COFFEE AND . . .

With a cup of Dunkin' Donuts' coffee in one hand
and a delicious dunkable donut in the other, a fella'
can face whatever the world has to dish out.

As difficult as it may seem, New Englanders are human, too. Like most Americans, we often need a jolt in the morning to appreciate a fine sunrise or get through a standard New England gray day. With a cup of Dunkin' Donuts coffee in one hand and a delicious dunkable donut in the other, a fella' can face whatever the world has to dish out.

In 1946, on the outskirts of Boston, William Rosenberg made his regular stops with his coffee truck to area construction sites. Rosenberg, however, was a man with a plan. He saw the future of donuts and wanted to be a part of the whole (bad pun) thing. He began the Open Kettle in Quincy, and two years later it became the first Dunkin' Donuts shop. In 1955, the first franchise agreement was signed, and the donut empire began.

New Englanders thrive on the deep, rich coffee and the rich morsels served fresh at each shop. "And where are those little shops," you might ask. The answer is simple, "Everywhere!" Just about every city and town in the wondrous region of the Northeast has at least one. They dot the landscape like oases in the desert. Weary travellers and fast-paced businessmen alike, stand in rapidly-moving lines for a cup of "joe" and a "sinker with a handle."

In 1966, Dunkin' Donuts University was created. No, it's not a new Big East school with a great hockey team, but it's a great way to keep in touch with your classmates in high schools and colleges across the country.

In 2,000, Dunkin' donuts celebrated its 50th anniversary by opening its 5,000th store in Bali, Indonesia. Now, you can wake up in countries around the world and still have a taste of New England.

Oh, a little tip on coffee lingo in New England . . . "coffee and" refers to a cup of coffee AND something to go with it. In a Dunkin' Donuts shop, that is anything from a donut or a donut munchkin (a donut hole), to a breakfast sandwich. A "regular coffee" (as opposed to an irregular coffee) is coffee with cream and sugar added.

One of my favorite Dunkin' Donut experiences occurred when I returned to New England after a thirty-year absence. My wife had found the home of our dreams, and we were getting ready to sign the papers to move in. It was early morning, and the sun was trying to find a crack in the eastern sky. We drove to the local Dunkin' Donuts in Portsmouth, New Hampshire. We were third in line. We snatched up a bag of oven-fresh donuts and two cups of regular coffee and headed down to the seawall. Some of the others at the shop apparently had the same thought in mind, for we all met where the ocean meets the shore to watch the sunrise and a formation of Canada geese on the horizon.

We blew the steam from our cups and licked the jelly from our lips. You just can't do any better than that.

WRITERS FROM THE REGION

Stephen and Tabitha King of Bangor, Maine are exceptional fiction writers. Son, Joe Hill, in Exeter, New Hampshire, also wields a pen.

When I began to assemble the various topics for this book, Child Bride became more and more excited. "Don't forget this!" or "You can't overlook that!" or "People really need to know about . . ." were statements heard quite frequently as I added a little each day to the text. One topic she was very firm on was New England writers. I told her how complex that topic would be . . . fiction versus non-fiction; living versus deceased authors, male versus female; poets versus prose; etc. etc. Still, C.B. was relentless. Okay, so now you appreciate my problem. In an effort to make my wife happy, I am choosing a few authors from each state whose works stand out. Please understand, omissions don't mean I haven't read or don't care for particular authors , and inclusions don't mean these folks are true literary geniuses. They're just my picks. Fair enough?

Stephen and Tabitha King of Bangor, Maine are exceptional fiction writers. Their son, Joe Hill, in Exeter, New Hampshire, also wields a pen. That family has a wonderful knack of scaring the reader skinless with tales of horror and intrigue. Henry Wadsworth Longfellow, born in Portland, could be considered the all-encompassing New England writer of timeless prose and poetry that will never cease to bring enjoyment. Edna St. Vincent Millay of Camden won a Pulitzer Prize for her poetry. From love sonnets to great stuff for kids, her material is simply enchanting. Booth Tarkington called Kennebunkport home. Also, a Pulitzer Prize winner, he is included on The Modern List of the 100 Best Novels.

Like your poetry just a little bit off the wall? You may wish to sample the works of e.e.cummings of North Conway, New Hampshire. Brendan DuBois, of Dover writes intriguing mysteries using the region as his backdrop. Born in Exeter, John Irving might be considered the state's greatest novelist. If you like your novels a lot on the eerie side, slip stealthily into Portsmouth's Dean Koontz. Nearly every high school kid has read and enjoyed J.D. Salinger of Cornish, New Hampshire. Wicked good stuff! Something controversial? Try Rye's Dan Brown.

Rhode Island has its share of serious writers. Here are a few I truly enjoy . . . if you you like your mysteries rich and juicy, curl up with Mary

Higgins Clark from Newport. Also from there is James Fenimore Cooper. Great early American literature! Peter Farrelly from Pawtucket wrote some very funny screenplays. Ever sing 'the Battle Hymn of the Republic'? Julia Ward Howe from Sunset Ridge wrote the words. Henry Wadsworth Longfellow of Newport was a terrific early American poet. Want some icy horror? Try Providence's H.P. Lovecraft. Want some simply witty verse? Try Ogden Nash. Scary verse? Kick back with Providence's Edgar Allen Poe. And, don't forget, Thornton Wilder was a Pulitzer Prize winner.

Like your fiction think, rich and luscious? Try Greenwich, Connecticut's Howard Fast. Norwalk gave us Evan Hunter (a.k.a. Ed McBain). Solid page-turning mysteries! William Manchester of Middletown wrote some superb biographies. Remember "Death of a Salesman?" Roxbury's Arthur Miller wrote it. Eugene O'Neil of New London also won a Pulitzer. Philip Roth of Litchfield County wrote "Good-Bye Columbus!" Tom Tryon from Hartford wrote some serious thrillers. Oh, Mark Twain called Hartford home, too.

Vermont is not to be denied. How about the great New England poetry of Robert Frost? Want some terrific popular fiction? Try Julia Alvarez. Stories of personal intrigue? Sample David Mamet.

Massachusetts has a number of authors I've enjoyed. Here's a short list; Luisa May Alcott, Isaac Asimov, Robert Benchley, Emily Dickinson, T.S. Eliot, Ralph Waldo Emerson, Ben Franklin, Nathaniel Hawthorne, Jack Kerouac and Herman Melville.

There you go, C.B., I hope you liked it.

THE ART OF SHOVELING

Let's explore some of the aesthetics of shovelling.

There are those who merely shovel snow. There are those who are true artisans of the craft. Most who wield the blade know, but are reluctant to share the various elements involved in shoveling. Now, let's explore some of the aesthetics of shoveling.

Certainly, stance and rhythm are extremely important. Position of the feet should approximate shoulder-width. (Envision David Ortiz at the plate.) Once comfortable, the shoveler should move forward one-half step at a time (begin with either foot). The removal of snow should follow the same progression (scrape, lift, toss, step, step) until the project is complete. Moving with a waltz tune in mind is about the correct speed.

Once the basics are learned, the shoveler may want to explore one or more of several truly eye-pleasing strokes. Water density, type and depth of snow should have a definite influence on the style chosen.

My personal favorite is the "herringbone" stroke. In it, the shoveler proceeds at an angle along the walk or driveway. Each patch is at a 45-degree angle to the surface. Each swatch is approximately 18" in length. When one tour is finished, the shoveler returns to complete the next pass adjacent to the first. The herringbone leaves a line of wonderfully precise corners framing the designated area.

The "candy cane" is very similar in appearance to the herringbone. It's similarly angled, but the shoveler completes one full swatch of the walkway. He turns and does the next in the opposite direction. Here, the samba may be preferred to the waltz.

"Stripping" is done in long, plow-like moves. The shoveler's blade never leaves the surface of the area, except at the end of each strip. One-half blade to the snow is recommended. The "empty" half catches the snow spilling in that direction. The shoveler may want to utilize a march step here.

"Cross-hatching" is an advanced and complicated maneuver. Essentially, it's stripping being alternated in a north-south to east-west rotation. One full strip is completed by the accomplished shoveler before the next. This approach is not recommended for novices, as extra march steps can easily destroy the cadence of a rookie blader.

New Englanders instinctively know what type and depth of snow should be attempted with the particular shovelling stroke. I'm not sure if it would ever be a hit, but I have envisioned a reality show titled, "Shovelling with the Stars!" I think it could be a goer.

WHERE TO PUT IT

Shovelers need to guard against the euphoria that accompanies the shoveling completed after the first storm, or two, or three.

Once you've chosen a proper shoveling technique (This, of course, will take one or two small storms to master.), the next step is finding a suitable locale in which to store the snow you have just cleared. The first few storms are usually a facile venture. Just slide the snow to the edge of your drive or walkway and pile it up.

Now, this presents a problem. Any true New Englander will tell you that. You see, by piling the white stuff up at the rim of what you have shoveled, you begin to form a wall. "No big deal," you say. No, not at first. But if Mother Nature turns fickle (as she is prone to do) on those of us who dwell shy of the Great White North, we may just have several storms waiting in the wings. Then, the berm you have created becomes a dreaded wall from keeping your walk clear.

That three-inch dusting could, in short order, become a three-foot wall! The next would make the wall four feet, and so on. So, true shovelers will tell you to hurl each bladeful toward the center of your yard (or your neighbor's), if you are close by and he's not looking.

Shovelers need to guard against the euphoria that accompanies the shoveling completed after the first storm, or two, or three. It's winter in New England, remember? The snow comes down until after your taxes are due. Many a spring bonnet has become a parka's hood when the skies turn to iron gray.

Once you have begun to create your mounds in the center of your yard, you need to be aware that those mounds will begin to obscure your vision from your windows. This is the first step toward a full-fledged case of cabin fever. Many a New Englander will tell you of those horrendous winters when the snow fell with a vengeance. The snow piled up to the second floors, and then some. On those occasions, New England bladers become creative.

Many enjoy a little sweet revenge at the snow plow trucks by tossing out shovelfuls of snow into the street (excluding yours truly, of course). This is usually done in the dark of night. It is usually accompanied by the "duck and look" to see if any neighbors have heard the sounds of your scraping shovel. A neighbor of mine recounted how he and the plowman had a running game of "shovel it out and push it back," until the plowman finally caved. One small win for shovelers; one giant victory for shovelkind!

"Hey, I'm plowing it the best I can. Where exactly would you like me to put it."

The answer to that question is as colorful as a New England sunset in autumn. Sadly, I can't print it here.

Another solution is to find a friend with a pick-up truck to haul away your snow. This venture is usually frowned upon because it means shoveling the same snow twice. New Englanders pride themselves as being staunchly against wasted motion. This plan certainly flies in the face of not wasting mo tion.

Other solutions include: the gigantic snowball, the use of a flame thrower, and the employment of a gargantuan conveyor belt to turn your garage into an igloo. There is a perfect solution, however.

Keep the plow truck driver happy (this may include the purchase of a bottle of his favorite beverage). Drop a few subtle hints regarding your purchase. Then, maybe, just maybe, he might turn up after his street shift to push the snow from your driveway down the street to someone who is less generous. (By the way, snow plow drivers usually have their blades mounted in September . . . Hey, you never know.)

HIKING NEW ENGLAND

I'm talking about a walk where the air is sweet, the birds are singing, and the sights are breathtaking.

Get yourself a walking stick. Any old firm, twigless branch that can fit nicely into the palm of your hand that touches the ground is perfect. Throw on some decent walking shoes (no, ladies, high heels won't cut it), and you're ready to take a walk. It doesn't matter where you go in New England; almost any place is a great spot for a hike.

First of all, let's consider the word "hike." I think it scares folks; I think it conjures up images of military expeditions with full packs and lots of sweat. I'm not talking about that kind of hike here. I'm talking about a kinder, gentler sort of amble. I'm talking about a stroll, solitary or otherwise, through wooded hills, aside scenic lakes or ponds, and over gentle slopes. I'm talking about a walk where the air is sweet, the birds are singing, and the sights are breathtaking. Ladies and gentlemen, I'm talking about taking a walk in New England!

A hike doesn't necessarily mean a long trek measured in double-digit mileage. A walk in this region could be as long as it takes to clear the head, to appreciate the landscape, to exercise the legs or to simply get away from the mother-in-law for a while. I can't imagine a better spot to go for a jaunt than this fair region. Pick a season. Chart a course. Now, go!

If you like urban ambling, many areas in metropolitan New England are for you. Aside from the Freedom Trail in Boston, most are not marked. You have to be a bit adventuresome here. Check the historic markers. Gawk at the shop windows. Do a little people-watching (not too much, people will wonder what you're up to). Enjoy the day. Stop in a coffee shop. There are thousands of them here. Pick up a personal treasure, and then head home to admire your purchase. It's great fun. Two great little towns to experience the perfect stroll are Portsmouth, New Hampshire and Newburyport, Massachusetts. The smiles in both places are free, and they are abundant.

If you live near the coast, how lucky are you! I don't know anyone who tires of taking in a gentle sea, or watching the waves crash against the rocks. And, just about everyone likes to dip his or her pinkies into the surf, don't they? Top off you day with a cup of clam chowdah at a shop near the Marginal Way in York, Maine. Now, you, my friend, have had a very full day.

How about an autumn amble in the country? Run your hand along a stone wall. Stop and gaze at a distant church steeple. Visit a roadside fruit and vegetable stand. Sample an apple. Your taste buds will thank you for it.

Here's one I'll bet you haven't tried. Find an abandoned set of train tracks (make sure its abandoned), and head off along them in the winter during, or just after a slight snow. You can't get lost. The tracks will take you as far as you want to go, and your footprints will tell you your destination home.

Feeling a bit more courageous? Try to trek up Mt. Washington, or along the Appalachian Trail, or through Franconia Notch. Now, those are hikes, but well worth the effort. The views are spectacular, and the feeling of personal accomplishment is a definite high. Feeling even a bit more courageous? You may want to join the Appalachian Mountain Club (AMC). You can log your treks to the tops of the 100 tallest mountains in New England. What will you receive for your efforts? Self-satisfaction, a certificate (worth framing), and a subscription to AMC Magazine! Pretty nifty, huh?

Take a walk around your block. Stop and visit a neighbor who may be sitting on his or her front porch. Enjoy a game or two of cribbage.

Enjoy New England up close and personal. Take a hike, Jack!

WALDEN POND

Walden Pond is located not very far from Concord Bridge, the site of the famous "shot heard round the world." A reproduction of Thoreau's house stands in the same location as the original.

I was just daydreaming as I gazed from my office window, located on the second floor of my home in Hampton, New Hampshire. It is early spring, but I can easily count at least six shades of green on the trees which form a fine tapestry of majesty. The other day, three wild turkeys crossed the road at my front door and strolled across my yard. And, although I haven't caught one yet, I have it on good authority that the salmon are returning to rivers and streams of the region. Yes, the splendor that once was the region has returned in full. Perhaps, just perhaps, those of us in New England would have found out that progress doesn't always enhance our lives, but having a conscience certainly didn't hurt matters. The conscience of which I speak is Henry David Thoreau.

He was born on July 12, 1817, in Concord, Massachusetts. As a child, he was keenly aware of the natural beauty of the region and took long walks in the countryside to explore and enjoy. He went to Harvard and returned home to begin a career as a writer. His career choice may not have endeared him greatly to his family, who had hoped that he would eventually take the reins of the family's pencil-making business.

Thoreau taught school, did some surveying, but it may be safe to say that his passion was to commune with nature. In 1845, he designed and built a small house on the shores of Walden Pond. He lived in this home for over two years and drew heavily from this experience to write Walden. The theme of the book is dedication to nature.

Walden Pond is located not very far from Concord Bridge, the site of the famous "shot heard round the world."   A reproduction of the Thoreau house stands in the same location as the original. Nearby is a small statue of the man. In the grand scheme of things, the area, now a national Historical Landmark, is not very large at all. The entire location, including the surrounding woods, is a mere 2,680 acres. What strikes me as being truly remarkable is the impact that this humble man in this primitive location had on the world.

The pond is a calming place to visit. Yes, you can swim or walk your dog there, but you may just wish to walk the shore and reflect on the sights and sounds of the natural world around you.

After your visit to Walden Pond, you may wish to take a short drive to the Sleepy Hollow cemetery nearby. Henry's grave is located there. Oddly enough, the man may have had much more human company after his death than while he was alive. As you drive away after having enjoyed yourself, and I'm sure you will have, you may want to whisper a simple thanks to Henry. After all, he helped to make this grand day possible.

CHILD BRIDE COMES
TO NEW ENGLAND

How was I to know that she would fall madly in love with the place and want to move there after retirement?

I know . . . I know . . . conventional thinking holds that people should retire from the cold weather and move to a warmer southern or western environment. Apparently, that makes me somewhat akin to a salmon swimming downstream. You see, I left New England some thirty years ago to spend most of my adult life deep into south Texas and Las Vegas. A decade ago, I met Child Bride. She wanted to see the land of my roots and meet my relatives. I, thinking it would be wonderful short vacation, readily agreed to the idea. How was I to know that she would fall madly in love with the place and want to move there after retirement? I tried to play Devil's advocate.

"Honey, the skies are gray for more than half the year."

"Have you seen what the sun does to stop signs here in Sin City?" Child Bride asked, eyes aflutter. "It turns them pink."

"And, it snows," I said shivering. "There's always lots and lots of snow."

"Yes, won't it be wonderful?" Child Bride's face gazed skyward. Her beatific smile exuded warmth. "I just know I'm going to love shoveling."

The last time she felt ice was when she put ice cubes in a glass for lemonade.

"A lot of the time, it's just going to be the three of us alone in the house all winter."

"Three of us?" she asked, perplexed.

"Yes, you, me and cabin fever."

"Aw, sweetie, it will give us plenty of time to snuggle."

"Yeah, with your ice cold feet planted firmly against my back," I mumbled.

"Oh, it will be great," Child Bride said, ever so demurely. "There will be plenty of foliage to see in the fall; long walks along the beach on summer nights; and trips to Boston for plays, shopping, cultural events and Red Sox games."

"Red Sox," I asked, incredulously. "You'd sit through a Red Sox game?"

"He's got the cutest dimples . . . I mean he almost won the American League batting championship, didn't he?"

"You mean you really want to live the rest of your live in tropical southern New Hampshire? It will be more than a little change for you. Remember, people up there only use a 25-letter alphabet. The r's are optional."

"Sweetie, if I can understand you most of the time everyone else will be a cake walk."

Hundreds of New England transplants in Glitter Gulch tried to reason with her, but she was adamant. We were headed to the great Northern Empire. They just couldn't understand why we would leave all of that sun.

I must admit, she has adapted well. We've checked out the foliage; attempted fishing the North Atlantic from shore; gone on a lighthouse tour; picked apples in an orchard; and made friends with all of our terrific neighbors. The biggest thrill for Child Bride, however, was being named First Mate on the S.S. Buyabunch; it cruises the region in search of exceptional garage sales. We set sail every Saturday morning at the crack of dawn.

Child Bride's birthday is coming soon, and I have a special gift in mind for her . . . A hot-air balloon trip over the countryside or a brand new, super, deluxe, forest green, Teflon-coated snow shovel. I know she's really going to thank me for it. You're right. The balloon trip is the better choice.

THE NEW BIRD ON THE BLOCK

*The bird is really enjoying itself. The monks have
built their huge stick monasteries (sorry, couldn't resist)
in trees and telephone poles in some numbers.*

When you think of the birds of New England, a few immediately (maybe a few seconds after "immediately") come to mind. The turkey . . . Pilgrims . . . first Thanksgiving. True, right? The blue jay . . . year-round resident . . . loves the bird feeder in the backyard. Sure. The pigeon . . . painter of statues. I'm sure everyone has his or her own list. Quite honestly, I don't know how many species of birds live in this special land we call New England; I do know that bird watchers never seem to want for winged creatures to observe. There is, however, a relative newcomer to the New England skies, and it is vying for attention. Drum roll please . . . the monk parakeet. Okay, stop with the drums!

Here's the myth" In the late 1800's a merchant schooner was bound for Boston from ports in South America. The captain of the vessel had two monks that he was bringing back to the wife he hadn't seen in two years. A terrible winter storm smashed the ship against the rocks near Bridgeport, Connecticut. All aboard were lost, save the two parrots. The numbers of their offspring continue to flourish.

Yes, that was the myth. The real story is far less romantic. In the late 1960's, the monk parakeet took up residence in Connecticut. No one seems to know if one flew out a kitchen window, escaped from a pet shop or simply liked to follow the coast up from South America. So far, our new feathered friend doesn't seem to be doing anything disruptive to the environment. Apparently, it is fond of the insurance business and has chosen to take up residence in areas around Hartford.

The bird is really enjoying itself. The monks have built their huge stick monasteries (sorry, couldn't resist) in trees and telephone poles in some numbers. These mound-shaped structures can be anywhere from four to six feet in width. The bird is a messy housekeeper, but a real party animal having loud, raucous get-togethers long into the night. Monks fly, but seldom for long distances. My guess is that they travel only as far as the next party.

Their snack food seems to be insects and insect larvae. It is not clear if they are connoisseurs of fine wine, although there is a Gray Monk wine bottled in California.

So far, the monk parakeet is a welcome addition to the New England bird scene. There is no evidence yet as to whether the bird has learned to speak with a distinctive accent or if it has become a full-fledged member of Red Sox Nation. Stay tuned, America!

SUMMER THEATERS
IN NEW ENGLAND

. . . nothing is as mellow as New England summer theatre.

New Englanders love summer. They look forward to the season with as much anticipation as a fifteen year-old looks forward to a driver's license. They relish the days and shed as many clothes as community laws allow. Neighbors greet neighbors over stone walls, and the smells of things delicious from back deck grills permeate the air.

The nights are equally as sweet. The days are just a little longer, so the glow of the western sun keeps the dark away long enough for an extra game of kick-the-can or hopscotch on a sidewalk. The evenings are as delicious and as mellow as a fine wine. Speaking of mellow, (I wasn't, but I'll take any segway I can find) nothing is as mellow as New England summer theater. Nothing at all.

There are several great venues throughout the region. Here are a few to enjoy: The Ogunquit Playhouse in Maine has been cranking out great summer productions since 1937. It is termed "America's Foremost Summer Theater," and for good reason. Great actors and great productions have been coming to this area of New England for nearly 70 years. The Who's Who list stretches from the Barrymores to Sally Struthers and then some. Though ownership has changed over the years, the support of the community and its patrons has not.

Take two-pre-Revolutionary barns; put them together, and what do you have? The first Dorset Theatre is in Dorset, Vermont. It was built in 1929. In 2001, it came down and a wonderful 21st century building now houses terrific professional productions. This town has its origins some 150 years ago when "summer people" came to the area to retreat from the hectic pace of the day. Folks, the pace hasn't gotten much easier, but Dorset is still a magical place to go to enjoy the inns, festivals and especially the theater.

If you like your theater with the tang of salt air, there's no better place to enjoy it then at Prescott Park in Portsmouth, New Hampshire. For over thirty years, folks have been taking in great productions as passing fishing boats wend their way from their nearby harbor berths and out to sea. There is no fixed admission price, but don't be fooled by the minimal cost . . . the productions are first rate.

Okay, so you've savored Tanglewood; you've feasted on the visual treats of the Norman Rockwell Museum, but you still want more. What do you do? You make a beeline to the Colonial Theatre in downtown Pittsfield, Massachusetts. For over a century, this "architectural gem" is in the heart of the Berkshires has been producing fine shows in a setting of pure elegance. The ornate décor of a bygone era is perfect for relaxing and enjoying any presentation, and the acoustics are simply unbeatable. Of all of the great theaters built at the turn of the 20th century, it is one of only a dozen still standing and operating.

The smallest state in the union is not small on entertainment. Not by a long shot! The Stadium Theatre in Woonsocket, Rhode Island is a must for anyone who appreciates great theater and great music. Located in the heart of the Blackstone Valley, this theater was built in 1926 and is simply a grand place to be grandly entertained. Having ceased operations in 1970, the "Save Our Stadium" committee was formed in 1991. That labor of love produced the great enterprise that flourishes today.

A mere stone's throw from New York (if you have the arm of a Red Sox centerfielder) is New Canaan, Connecticut. Located outdoors in Irwin Park, the productions are top notch and the atmosphere is friendly. From Shakespeare to Broadway, the place is a theatergoer's delight.

There are more great theater experiences in New England . . . lots more. They're waiting for you this summer. So, what are you waiting for? Go!

THE GREAT ATLANTIC CABLE

*At one point, a whale became entangled
in the cable and had to be removed.*

From 1837 – 1845, Samuel Morse was perfecting the electromagnetic tele-graph. The invention was the breakthrough in long-distance communication. It essentially linked communication across North America from the Atlantic to the Pacific. In 1844, communication was permanently established between New York and Philadelphia.

In 1866, America still did not have a telegraph communication link to Europe. Attempts had been made in 1857 and 1858, but they proved to be unsuccessful. The American Civil War caused a further delay. In July of 1866, the Atlantic Telegraph Company chartered the largest steamship in the world, the Great Eastern, along with four other ships and a combined crew of 500 to complete the 2,800 mile connection of heavy cable from Valencia, Ireland to Trinity Bay, Newfoundland. When this link was made, the age of worldwide communications began.

The cable was an engineering marvel. Throughout the entire process, a great number of problems arose. A perfected insulation material had to be employed. A hole as large as a pinprick could cause a major problem for the security of the line. Further, there were problems with the weather, rough seas, the topography of the ocean floor and near collisions of vessels and dis-putes over patents. At one point, a whale became entangled in the cable and had to be removed. A system of white, numbered buoys had to be laid to mark the exact path of the line.

Once the Atlantic Ocean was breached, telegraph operators were em-ployed to send and receive the communiqués. The operators lived a life simi-lar to that of a soldier. He swore an oath of service, was respectful both on and off duty, and had to maintain a reputation of skill and reliability. There were two operators on duty at all times at each station. One acted as a first of-ficer. Operators were considered to be professionals, and all communications were considered to be highly confidential. Women operators were still years away from the communications scene.

Every major city along the Eastern seaboard had a railway system. The telegraph lines usually paralleled the railway system. Each city needed tel-egraph operators in receiving stations to relay or transmit messages to the next station. The system of stations took some years to complete. The receiving station in Rye, New Hampshire was established in 1874. It is located on Atlantic Avenue (formerly Old Beach Road) directly east of the marker for the facility located on Route 1. It was the first link between Halifax, Nova Scotia and the United States, 3,104 miles from the Irish coast to Rye Beach. On June 6, the final link of cable was on American soil.

There was no official celebration to mark the historic event, but several hundred folks turned out on what was supposed to be the landing of the cable at Straw Point on Tuesday, July 14. Fog caused the postponement until the next day. Some of the crowd had left the area, but most reappeared some hours later. Work was begun on the Ambassador to bring the cable to shore. The task was completed about 9:00 p.m.

Leslies Illustrated Newspaper reported, "It was a dark night and the procession of boats with their lanterns formed a gloomy appearance as it (the boat attached to the rope leading the cable) moved through the stillness broken by the heave-ho of the cable hands and the wild uncouth songs with which they accompanied their clock-like motions as they worked along the ropes." A hundred-gun salute was issued by two small cannons borrowed from Kittery. Leslies goes on to say, "With a hearty Yankee cheer, the completion of the task was announced."

The greatest period of activity for the use of the cable occurred during World War I. According to William M. Varrell's Rye on the Rocks, "On Saturday, August 8, 1914, the Rye Cable Station established a record for transmissions, sending a total of 30,000 words. One of the fastest transmissions was a ten-second message between Rye and Berlin announcing the results of the Harvard-Yale football game.

The Old Cable House at Rye Beach, New Hampshire was in constant operation until 1921. Its closure marked the end of the Pioneer Era in international communication. Currently, the House is a summer tourist home.

MOUNT WASHINGTON

Most New Englanders know it simply as THE MOUNTAIN.

Keep in mind, Child Bride is from the West. She grew up in the middle of the Continental Divide and was on the set when John Wayne starred in many of those great cowboy shoot-em-ups of yesteryear. That being said, it really takes a lot to awe her (aside from me, I mean). Well, upon arrival to the Granite State, she scoffed up a wad of "must see" pamphlets at the local grocer/store and sat down that night to ponder them. She selected one.

"Hon, have you ever been to Mt. Washington?"

"Yep, it was about a hundred years ago, when I was a kid. Most New Englanders know it simply at THE MOUNTAIN. "

"Tell me about it."

"Okay," I said, and I did. I told her that coal-fired Cog Railway was nearly 140 years old, and how the train and cars were built on an angle to keep the ride as horizontal as possible.

I told her that on a clear day at the top, a person could look out over four states, see Quebec, actually see the Atlantic Ocean and glimpse at the Old Man of the Mountain when it actually had a face.

In my best theatrical voice, I informed her that the highest recorded winds in the world have been recorded there. They were 231 miles per hour.

I told her that from 1849 to now, at least 137 people had lost their lives on the mountain. There have been murders, plane crashes, train accidents, skiing accidents, climbing accidents, a carriage accident, and one person was even blown by the wind into another state.

I said that there are four distinct climates on the way to the top and that it may be sweltering at the base and snowing on top.

She gave me an "Aww, c'mon" kind of face.

"Really," I said. "You can hike up in shorts and go skiing once you get there."

I told her about the great fire of 1908 in which all of the buildings at the summit burned to the ground.

I told her that it is becoming a true rite of passage for 21st century drivers, who almost have to be surgically removed from their cars, to proudly display a bumper sticker that reads, "This car climbed Mt. Washington."

"And," I added, pausing for dramatic effect, "Tuckerman's Ravine at the Mountain is one of the steepest, most challenging ski slopes in the world."

I told her about the great trout fishing in nearby streams; added generous portions of information of other wildlife in the region; rolled into a great presentation about the spectacular museums of the mountain and the railway; rambled on about the spectacular drive to the top, and the fact that it crosses the Appalachian Train, and ended by saying that there are terrific restaurants in abundance nearby.

"That settles it," she said, stashing the brochures into her purse. "We're going up there first thing in the morning."

"I'm game," I said, "but tell me, what is it that intrigues you so much about the place . . . the weather . . . the winds . . . the view? My guess is that it's the great sweat you'll build up on the hike to the top."

"The car keys are on the kitchen table," she said demurely, and went into the other room to watch 'Wheel of Fortune.'

I think I heard her say something about hiking and pigs flying, but I'm probably wrong.

THE LITTLE ENGINE THAT COULD

*The Cog Railway is the first and oldest
cog railway system in the world.*

In 1858, Sylvester marsh appealed to the State of New Hampshire to build a railroad to the summit of Mt. Washington. Legislators laughed and told him he should amend his request and build a railway to the moon. One July 3, 1869, the Cog Railway was built and the first engine, 'Old Peppersass' began trundling passengers to the summit. That was no easy feat. The climb to the top of the mountain is 6,288 feet, and the grade is 37.41%. In August of that year, certain all of the kinks had been ironed out, President Ulysses S. Grant and his family made the journey to the top.

Not only was the trek arduous, the equipment for the train had to be invented! Father and son, Herrick and Walter Aiken, from Franklin, New Hampshire, had that responsibility. To take the engine and all that was needed, they employed a team of oxen to travel the twenty-five mile journey to Bretton Woods, and another six miles through heavy forest to the base of the mountain.

The Cog Railway is the first and oldest cog railway system in the world. Everything about the system is unique, including the engine. It and the coal car are angled in such a way as to keep them as nearly perpendicular to the track as possible. Standing in the passenger car, one can lean forward at a severe angle with no fear of falling face first.

No one will tell you that you should take your seat as far from the locomotive as possible. You should, unless of course, you enjoy the taste of cinders as they rain down on the back of your car. In the course of a trip up the mountain, one train will consume 1,000 gallons of water and one ton of coal.

Near the summit, the tracks cross the Appalachian Trail. Hikers and train travelers have been exchanging friendly waves for years, although the hikers have been known to "moon" the train. There are no reports of an even exchange being given back from the train.

The view from any seat on the passenger car is breathtaking. On a clear day, the Atlantic Ocean, Quebec, and four states are visible from Mount Washington. At the summit, the seventy passengers carried up in one passenger car can take in the Mt. Washington Observatory Museum or head to the Sherman Adams building for refreshments. While the passengers are busy enjoying the summit, the brakeman and the engineer flip the backs on each of the seats in the passenger car, so riders will be able to face down the mountain for the return trip.

The railway is open year round in all kinds of weather. It is a definite treat to take the trip during any and all of the four seasons to experience the astounding changes in the landscape.

When the last whistle is blown and the train arrives safely at the platform at the base of the mountain, the passengers can now take in the gift shop and museum at Marshfield Station. Many will stop and turn around for one last glimpse of "the railway to the moon." While they are looking up, they most certainly will see the next contingent of passengers standing at the station. In a few moments, when the train has been prepared, they most certainly will hear the engineer call out, "All aboard!"

Take the trip. It's an awe-inspiring experience.

THE GREAT MOLASSES FLOOD

The once-chilled mass of molasses had expanded in the tank, and the tank had exploded. Veterans back from the war said that the popping rivets sounded exactly like machine gun fire.

There are some stories, like some photographs, that one would rather not dwell on, but you simply can't help yourself. The Great Molasses Flood is one of those stories for me.

The year was 1919. The Great War was over. The Red Sox had won the World Series in 1918. All was right with the world. Boston was teeming with life, particularly at the harbor.

January 15th was a beautiful day. There was no snow on the ground. The temperature was hovering around 40 degrees . . . a preview of spring, maybe, but certainly a January thaw day.

A few days earlier, 2,300,000 gallons of molasses had been delivered to Boston from Puerto Rico. It was thought to be secure in a tank that was 50 feet high and 240 feet around. The tank was made of steel and held tighter by heavy rivets. It was located on Copp's Hill just above the harbor in what is now the Italian North End. The molasses was going to be used to make ammunition, rum and great topping for pancakes.

Traffic in the area was heavy. Ponderous trucks and large, cumbersome wagons filled the streets in the harbor region. Folks were busy. It was a great day to be outside. Everyone seemed to be taking advantage of the terrific weather. About noon, many workers were taking their lunch outdoors. At 12:30, folks heard a groan and then a muffled roar. The once-chilled mass of molasses had expanded in the tank, and the tank had exploded. Veterans back from the war said that the popping rivets sounded exactly like machine gun fire. One section of the tank was blown across Commercial Street taking out the supporting structure of the El. The train was nearing the location and rumbled to a stop just before reaching the molasses wave. Another piece of the tank crashed into a freight house directly behind some of the workers who had been lunching only moments before.

The cascade of molasses was 15 feet high and weighed over 14,000 tons as it rolled across streets and into houses. It collapsed at least one home, crushing an occupant. The wave was estimated to be travelling about 35 miles per hour. So fast was the goo going that it caught three children walking home from school. One boy "surfed" the molasses for several feet until he was rolled in it like a pebble. When he was found, he was thought to be dead and placed on the ground beside the bodies. He was very much alive, but his sister had been killed.

Wagons, horses and bodies were swept by the brown tide down the hill and into the harbor. The final count was 21 dead, 150 injured, and numerous horses had been killed. A great part of the glob rolled across Commonwealth Street and into the waters of the harbor. It took several days using high-pressure hoses from fire boats firing salt water to clean up the major portion of the mess. The problem with the substance, however, was that it got all over everything in greater Boston, from the train tracks to the telephone poles. Everything seemed to be sticky for the better part of that winter.

There is no plaque in the area to mark the site of the incident. The stains of the second floors of houses coated by the molasses have disappeared over time. Curiously, there are still reports that on particularly hot days in summer, a faint trace of molasses can be detected in the air.

Personally, I like my disasters on a much smaller scale. Something akin to "Honey, I just spilled the maple syrup on the table! Where are the paper towels?" That's just about all the spill I can handle.

THE SEASONS OF NEW ENGLAND

I missed the truest clock that keeps me attuned to my life and my world . . . the four distinct seasons of the year.

There is a small park on the shores of Portsmouth Bay. The view isn't breathtaking. The park is, however, calming, settling and serene. From this slightly elevated slip of land, one can take in three lighthouses, one of which was built by the British in revolutionary times; an ancient rescue station; a marina complete with assorted small boats, and a chain of islands fading off into the Atlantic. On the slight cliff overlooking this vista, someone has thoughtfully placed a black metal frame, with the silhouette of a painter posing next to it, in which to take the view at whatever particular angle one may choose . . . in the weather of one's choice . . . in the season of one's choice.

I've been away from New England for more years than I care to consider, and it wasn't until I returned that I realized I missed the truest clock that keeps me attuned to my life and my world . . . the four distinct seasons of the year. I left in search of the sun, and I found it. What I didn't find was the gentle progression through the seasons that seems to offer a fellow purpose in life.

Child Bride and I have taken many drives to Prescott Park in Portsmouth. Each time we go, I stand in front of that frame and look out over the waters. The irony of that framed piece of the world seems to be that the constant change of the panorama offers one constancy in life. That, in and of itself, may be the greatest gift New England has to offer.

The weather may be a formidable challenge here; no one knows that better than someone stuck on Route 128 in a blinding nor'easter at what should be rush hour. The weather is not all there is to New England. I believe that the weather is only representative of the season. It helps us to appreciate our frailties. It helps us to see that we are in a relationship with our neighbors. After all, we're all in this life together, aren't we?

I don't know which season began the life cycle, but each offers something different to the citizen blessed enough to be a member of the grand community of New England. Interestingly enough, no season begins or ends exactly when it is supposed to according to the calendar. A surprise snowstorm in May; a shirt sleeve day in February; a heavy frost in early October; or a ferocious gale in August remind us that even our best plans are man-made. New

Englanders are very aware that we can take nothing for granted. We can't hurry spring by taking down the storm windows; we can't assume life will grant us favors simply because we wish it to be so.

New Englanders, I believe, don't just age as the seasons progress one to the next. We mature. We grow from the experience of the season past while we're living in the present and preparing for the future. We watch our children grow. We experience anew their thrills and landmark events through the days, months, and years on our planet in the world we call New England. We do this in the same way that our parents and grandparents did as they progressed in life through the seasons of the region.

The gift we have is the time we know spend and share in New England. The reality is that the life here is constant, yet ever-changing. The knowledge that we gain is that which we glean from our experiences through the years. Life in New England is wonderful!

MAKE WAY FOR DUCK BOATS

They are the perfect touring vehicle for Boston. That's right! On any given day, you can take a DUCK boat tour of Boston.

When I was a lad, back at the dawn of time, a hurricane slammed into Massachusetts and dumped tons of water into Main South Worcester. Like most areas of the region, it is a wonderful collection of hills and valleys. After this storm, however, the valleys were now lakes. Just about everything was under water. Help was needed desperately. That's when the DUCKs came in. Those big, beautifully ugly surplus vehicles left over from the invasion of Normandy saved the day.

After the war years, the DUCKs (Actually, they are the DUKWs – Designed Utility "amphibious" K "all-wheeled drive" W "two powered rear-axled vehicles. Call 'em DUCKs, okay?) were almost cut up for scrap metal. Somebody thought better of the idea, and the big critters have been a notable part of the New England scene ever since.

Yes, they are used in emergencies. These giant creatures get the job done if the need arises following a ferocious nor'easter or snarling hurricane. Of late, however, these babies are getting lots of show time because of the sudden rash of championships in the region. (You may recall that the Patriots have won four Super Bowls recently. Oh, yes, if memory serves me, the Red Sox and Bruins have won a little something as well.)

You won't find them wearing the Army olive green any longer. They're party animals now! The DUCKs come in everything from bright red to baby blue . . . and every color in between. But even without the new color schemes, you can't miss 'em. They are 31 feet long, nearly 8 feet wide, and over 9 feet tall. They weight over 7 tons! Heavy duty, eh?

They are the perfect touring vehicle for Boston. That's right! On any given day, you can take a DUCK boat tour of Boston. The drivers are witty and informative, and you get to look down on the traffic just before you plunge into the Charles. Every rider, at least for a moment, wishes he could own one, but the reality of parking one does present a bit of a problem.

Please indulge me a bit here if you will. The DUCKs don't have a tremendous part to play in my life, but the fact that they are still around chokes me up . . . just a little. You see, I can still see friends and neighbors . . . old folks and infants being taken to safety after that hurricane in the 50's. The DUCKs were truly life savers then.

Michael F. Bisceglia, Jr.

I was gone from the area for a number of years. Wouldn't you know it, the Sox won the World Series while I was out of town. For me, the vision of my team (hey, I'm a fan) receiving the adulation of Red Sox nation while cruising through the Boston streets and streams in a DUCK parade brought tears to my eyes.

Pretty special for me . . . yes, they are!

LIBRARIES CHANGE LIVES

If Main South had one redeeming feature, it was the library.
The Main South Branch Library wasn't much as libraries go.

Worcester, Massachusetts is a factory city. The dominant color of the sky and most of the buildings is gray. Much of the year, the weather ranges from cold to artic frigid. Statistics, news and census reports indicated that the Main South section of the city cornered the market on all that are negative: crime, disease and infant death, to name a few.

If Main South had one redeeming feature, it was the library. The Main South Branch Library wasn't much as libraries go, a former beauty salon wedged between a fish and chips store and an abandoned mansion. But to me, it was terrific. And, it was my library!

I only had to cross one street to get there. And, if I went down an alley, over a wall and up a fire escape, I could usually avoid the thugs who lurked on the corner next to Louie's Pharmacy.

The librarian was cast in a stereotypical mold; ageless after sixty, glasses hung about her neck, and a "shhh" that could drop a voice at sixty yards. Her only digression from the stereotype of yesteryear was that she had blue hair. Everyone knew that only fifth grade teachers were allowed to have blue hair.

The ancient floors at Main South were waxed, buffed and oiled until the glare caused blind spots if one stared too long. They also squeaked. I would often become so immersed in a story that my foot would begin keeping time to the war drums or the gait of the monster or whatever it was in the book which had captured my attention. Then a sobering "shhh" would be directed at me, and my foot would rest at ease until I was once again caught up in the story.

I read every book in the children's section of Main South, or at least every boy's book. Real guys didn't frequent the library; but if they did, they certainly didn't read books that were written by women or ones that came in pastel covers.

I owe much of my size, not my height, to the library, because that old library and the fish and chips store shared a common ventilating system. Whenever I really hunkered down with some space aliens or a marauding band of renegades, the desire for haddock and a slab of spuds would overpower me. Looking back, I wonder if anyone who frequented Bernie's Fresh Caught ever had the burning yen to read a book around mealtime.

I read my first dirty book at Main South. One day, walking through the adult section, I noticed a book lying open on the table. It was *The Jerry Geisler Story,* the tales of Errol Flynn's lawyer. The page was soooo hot! I sneaked it back to the children's area and continued. I knew my eyes were going to burn out of my head, but I just didn't care. In fact, I think I might have been the person who arrived at the idea of putting a small book inside of a larger one so that the reader appeared to be enjoying pure innocence. I discreetly showed that trick to a couple of less creative kids who promptly showed it to the rest of the world. The blue-haired librarian began finding tons of raw adult stuff wedged between the pages of The Hardy Boys. I believe she retired shortly thereafter.

I saw that old library last November, when I went back to Worcester for a wedding. Actually, I saw only the building. No longer a library, it had become a beauty shop once again. The guys still hang out in front of the Sunshine Health Food Store, formerly Louie's Pharmacy. And, oh yes, they all dawdle along with canes now, so the alley and the fire escape are no longer the recommended route of travel.

The weather is still brisk there in the Bay State. Bernie still makes outstanding fish and chips. He must drive the women in the beauty salon to total distraction. I just wonder if any of them have the urge to pick up a Mark Twain instead of an extra order of fries.

NEW ENGLAND-
STYLE HOTDOG BUNS

The shaved bun allows the holder of the Fenway (as in "ballpark") frank to be neatly and snugly placed in perfectly rectangular open frank boxes i.e., the type any vender will gladly serve you during a standard defeat of the Yankees.

The article could easily fall under the heading of: You learn something new everyday. I have to admit, I had no idea such a critter existed until Child Bride and I took up residence in New Hampshire some thirty years after I had left the glorious region of the northeast. We were at a dear friend's house in East Douglas, Massachusetts and were enjoying a backyard cookout.

"Look," she exclaimed. Her eyes were as big as saucers as she examined the Fenway frank nestled into the bun on her plate. "That's really something!"

I gazed into her plate expecting to see ancient hieroglyphics or at least a runic message carved into her potato chips.

"The hotdog buns are different," she said aghast. "They're not like the ones we had out west."

"Buns are buns," I said, certain of my simple declaration.

It turns out she was right. I guess I have to start paying attention to the little things in life.

First of all, the New England strain of the bun family is rich in eggs and butter. For the record, our buns are toasted. If you're watching your cholesterol intake, you may wish to settle for something watered down (maybe a New York-style bun).

The big difference . . . the obvious difference . . . the one I absolutely, positively missed, is that the sides of the New England-style hotdog bun are shaved! Apparently, (and I'm not a connoisseur of fine buns), every other bun in the western world (maybe the eastern, as well) has a rounded, individualized surface with a crust. For some mischievous reason, the buns we hold near and dear have a crust on top.

I've done my research on the little beauty, and I can't seem to find who should be credited (being "responsible" has the connotation of a shaved bun being a bad idea) with this sandwich engineering feat. My best guess, and this is only a guess, is that the shaved bun allows the holder of the Fenway (as in "ballpark") frank to be neatly and snugly placed in perfectly rectangular open frank boxes i.e., the type any vender will gladly serve you during a standard defeat of the Yankees. The fact that the item is squared and placed in a squared server allows for no rolling room. One does not want rolling room, for it allows for the desired culinary treat to wander off one's plate and onto the floor. The bun does certainly allow for plenty of room for mustard, relish (basic Fenway condiments) and catsup . . . and onions, if one so desires.

I posed the question regarding the unique style of New England bun to friends and family and received overwhelming enthusiastic answers ranging from: "Mrrflosrph." (I have no idea what was said over a mouthful of hot dog" to "No kidding? Huh! Pass the onions."

I'm not going to pursue the matter further. Let's just say that if you happen to be on Jeopardy and the big bonus answer at the end is "This shaved item neatly holds a dog in check," the correct question is "What is a New England-style hotdog bun?"

Thank you, now please pass the mustard.

SPRING FIX UP!

The event is possibly something akin to soldiers coming out of their shelters after the 'all clear' has been blown.

Spring doesn't march triumphantly into the Northeast. It seems to edge politely in after winter and goes almost unnoticed at first. The sun stays out a minute longer. The temperature goes up a degree. The snow recedes from the driveway at the rate of 1/16" per day.

Residents notice the changes, but they don't want to trust them. They don't want to have their hopes of the new season dashed by a surprise nor'easter. Remember, these folks are from Red Sox Nation. Even though we won the World Series in '04 and '07, we're still fragile.

Somebody finally breaks the ice and puts his nose outside the door. A neighbor sees him and follows suit. The event is possibly something akin to soldiers coming out of their shelters after the 'all clear' has been blown; they believe it is safe, but they're just really not sure. They look to the skies; they look at each other. They give one another a tentative smile.

The snow ebbs a bit more and the aftermath of winter becomes apparent. The snows and the winds of the season just having ended have left behind the wreckage of what was so beautiful before the first snows fell. Broken branches, roof shingles, assorted children's toys and much more seem to have conspired to turn gorgeous yards into what appears to be the remains of a ferocious battle.

Not only have the yards been assaulted, but the homes of the area have suffered as well. Paint work needs dire attention. Trimming needs to be replaced. Eaves and roofing require find tuning. Stonewalls need to be walked and reestablished. The list is seemingly endless.

There is no official date to regain control of the domains of New England, but suddenly you hear it. There's the rhythmic tapping of a hammer on a rooftop two doors down . . . a chainsaw is fired up across the street . . . ladders are clunked into position from the barn to the east. The elves of spring begin their toils. Pick-up trucks rumble from driveways and the survivors of winter meet at the local transfer station/dump, steaming Styrofoam cups in hand, with mound after mound of useless winter debris. They smile, nod knowingly and return to the labors of the season.

The chores of spring require a great deal of planning and terrific attention to detail. That's my specialty. I can plan to do work like nobody's business. I'm great at it. I can glance at a shaky banister and recognize in a heartbeat that it needs some attention. I can tell within a foot or two how long a wall is needing paneling. Yes, I am probably one of the best New England work planners of all time. If there was a hall of fame for folks of my ilk, my bust would hold a place of honor. After all, I probably hold some major league records for seeing the work needed on my property and planning to have it done.

Now, getting to actually repairing what needs to be repaired . . . that's another story. Oh, yeah, sure, I know the business end of a hammer. I'm not a complete rookie. I can tell you that a Phillips head screwdriver is used to fit into one of those little rascals with an "X" in its crown. Certainly, I know how to arrange tools neatly after a project is complete. But you have to understand, I'm a planner. I see a job that needs to be done. I plan for it. I schedule it. I make the calls to the pros who know how to efficiently tackle a project. I take bids. I hire. Yes, I am a planner.

Right now, I'm planning to be out the door and down the street when Child Bride starts looking for me to help repair the steps on the back porch!

THE NEW ENGLAND CIGAR

*. . . some of the finest blemish-free wrapper tobacco in the world
is grown right here in wonderful New England.*

There's nothing like it . . . a fine meal . . . a glass of mellow scotch . . . and a great New England cigar. No kidding, some of the finest blemish-free wrapper tobacco in the world is grown right here in wonderful New England.

Keep in mind, Native Americans in the region had pipe smoking rituals long before the advent of the colonists. The tobacco they smoked grew wild along the riverbanks. As America moved westward, the interest in the tobaccos of Connecticut grew as well.

Long lines of covered wagons, Conestoga Wagons - built in Lancaster, Pennsylvania, were the prime means of transportation. The lucky owners were provided with a box of fine cigars placed under the seat upon purchase. The cigars were most likely wrapped in tobacco from New England and came to be known as "stogies."

The tobacco is course and dark. Its seeds can be traced back to Cuba. It thrives in the late summer and early fall. Motorists driving through the region can easily see long lines of gauzy tents sheltering the plants.

Once the tobacco is harvested, it must be hung in large barns and allowed to dry (cure). This process can take up to two years. The product is not inexpensive. The cost is about $45 a pound.

The plants must be protected. Damage by hail, winds and extreme winters can destroy a crop.

Even though cigars may cause heart and lung damage, cigar smoking is enjoying a minor resurgence of late. In 1999, Massachusetts and Connecticut exported nearly 200 million dollars of the product.

A good cigar is not for everyone. But, if you are one of the breed who enjoys a quality smoke, chances are great that yours will be wrapped in a fine Connecticut leaf. So . . . light up . . . sit back . . . and enjoy!

IT'S A LITTLE KNOWN FACT

Toothpicks, earmuffs, and the first donut hole
maker were all invented in Maine.

Most every New Englander has an affinity for the television sitcom
Cheers. The cast of characters seems too real to us, probably because there
are little bits of each of them in each of us. My particular favorite is Cliff
Clavin: Mr. American Postman, Mr. Ladies' Man, and Mr. Encyclopedia of
Trivial Information. His standard, "It's a little know fact . . ." would simply
do me in. (I think I may have said exactly the same thing over the years.
Luckily, Carla Tortelli was never around to do me bodily harm.) So, as a
tribute to Cheers and to Cliff, here are some little known facts about New
England:

Toothpicks, earmuffs, and the first donut hole maker were all invented in Maine. The women in Maine were the first to exercise the right to
vote. Maine is the only state to have only one syllable in its name. Maine is
as big as the other five New England states put together. The first chartered
town, York, was established in 1641. The state flower is the pine cone.

Vermont gave us the open reel for fly fishing, potash, the rotary pump,
the electric railway, and the cast iron cooking oven. It is the smallest state in
population, and has the least amount of crime. Brattleboro produced the first
postage stamp in 1846. (I'm sure Cliff knew that.) Montpelier is the only state
capital without a McDonald's. Of the 13 original colonies, Vermont was the
first state admitted to the union. Snowboarding was developed there.

Vulcanized rubber, the sewing machine, the toll house cookie, the smi-
ley face, the rocket and the birth control pill all came from Massachusetts.
The Fig Newton was named after Newton, Massachusetts. The first zip code
was in Agawam, 01001. (Cliff probably knew that one, too.) The first basketball game was played in Springfield. The first public school was founded
in Dorchester. The official state dessert is the Boston cream pie. Titleist golf
balls are made in Achushnet.

In Hartford, Connecticut, you may not cross any street while walking on
your hands. The first hamburger came from Connecticut, as did the Polaroid
camera, the helicopter, and color television. Connecticut was the first state to
issue license plates for cars. Cattle branding began there. Cup sizing for bras
was introduced in that fair city. Pay telephones were invented and first used

in Hartford. One may not play Scrabble in Atwoodville while waiting for a politician to speak.

Rhode Island has the shortest state motto, "Hope." The longest professional baseball game (32 innings) took place in Pawtucket on April 19-20and June 23, 1981. The oldest and northernmost topiary garden is located in Portsmouth. In 1904, the first jail sentence was given for speeding. The culprit was going 15 mph. The oldest tavern in the country (the White Horse Tavern, built in 1673) is located in Newport. The nations' oldest carousel is located on Watch Hill.

Only one man ever played for the Boston Celtics, the Boston Bruins and the Boston Red Sox . . . John Kiley, the organist. George S. Parker, designer and manufacturer of some 29 board games, was born in Salem, Massachusetts in 1867.

It's a well known fact that there are tons of little known facts about New England. On any given day, you may hear one or two . . . particularly if you hang around with characters like Cliff Clavin.

For the record, the exterior shots of Cheers were taken of the Bull & Finch Pub located at 84 Beacon Street in Boston. You probably won't find Cliff there, but everybody does know his name.

NEW ENGLAND AMUSEMENT PARKS

One of the thrills I had as a boy was heading off to the
White City Amusement Park.

I lived for summer when I was a kid. Actually, I went into teaching for three reasons: June, July and August. One of the thrills I had as a boy was heading off to the White City Amusement Park on the shores of Lake Quinsigamond in Shrewsbury, Massachusetts. It was a great place.

It was chuck-filled with all kinds of stuff that was great fun for kids, but certainly would not pass any kind of safety requirements today. Oddly enough, I don't remember any kid complaining of anything more than a bruised ego from the bumper cars. The place was built in 1905 and dismantled in September of 1960. It was called a trolley park. There were several in New England. The idea was to keep commuters on the trolleys on the weekends, as well as during the week.

I wasn't around for some of the more spectacular earlier rides, but I do remember The Zip, a wild and wooly wooden roller coaster. There were a few rides that took patrons over, and sometimes into, the lake. And, there was a miniature railway that took kids through the woods, around the lake, and safely back to the platform all the while puffing smoke and ringing a bell as the engine chugged away. Talk about thrills! For the older crowd, there was a wonderful wooden dance pavilion built out over the lake, and each night featured an electric light show to dazzle the eye and make memories to last a lifetime. All that remains of the park now are some of the old wooden posts from the pavilion. That was from an era almost completely non-existent today.

I say "almost" because the amusement park at Lake Compounce in Bristol, Connecticut still welcomes thousands of patrons each and every summer. It has been doing so since 1846. It is the country's oldest continuously-operating amusement park. The park boasts many of the same rides as White City and much more. The Skyride, Ghost Hunt and Thunder Rapids are just a few.

Another charming old park still entertaining myriads of families is Santa's Village in Jefferson, New Hampshire. It has been around since 1952 and the kids still love to ride Rudy's Rapid Transit roller coaster, the Yule Log Flume, Santa's Skyway Sleigh and more. And, no visit would be complete without a few words with Ol' Saint Nick himself.

In my neck of the woods, there's Canobie Lake Park located in Salem

New Hampshire. It has been around since 1902 and boasts 47 rides. Included here are: the Starblaster, the Turkish Twist and the ever-popular Canobie Corkscrew.

There are at least a dozen amusement parks scattered throughout New England. There's even a Six Flags (I would really like to know the historical significance) in Agawam, Massachusetts. It used to be Riverside Park, a former trolley destination, but times change and so do the thrills.

I'm not going into detail here, but the region does not lack for summer excitement. The water rides, the wild animal attractions, antique railways fun (perfect for my speed) and event a mega-maze are all here.

My suggestion: Pack a picnic lunch, strap in the kiddies and be a kid again yourself. Enjoy the day. Enjoy the rides. Enjoy life in New England. They're memories you don't want to miss.

Michael F. Bisceglia, Jr.

TRADITIONAL MEALS OF NEW ENGLAND

It is those traditions which help to set New England apart from the rest of the country.

The Glorious Realm of the Northeast is rich in tradition. Quite possibly, it is those traditions which help to set New England apart from the rest of the country. One of the delicious traditions (pun intended) which we enjoy so well is our cooking. Here, it is not simply what is served, but when. Traditional meals fall on traditional days.

After extensive research (eating lots and lots of meals), I have found that Sunday might well be considered Ethnic Day. So many New Englanders have origins from outside of the United States. It is usually the Sunday noon meal (Lunch here is dinner. Dinner here is supper.) in which the favorite meals from the country of origin are served. It is common to walk down a street and smell corned beef and cabbage at one house, pasta with salsa d'Bisceglia next door and cipaille simmering in the house after that.

Monday evening is often given to devouring the leftovers from Sunday. It is true; most all dishes taste better the second time served. Monday night meals are not to be missed.

More often than not, Tuesday nights are given over to soups and stews. There is a myriad of delicious recipes which are brought to a delectable goodness on those evenings. Chowders, stews, broths and soups are served and relished by all New Englanders.

Wednesday night is spaghetti night. Not matter what your ethnic origins, Wednesday seems to be the day given over to that sumptuous repast. In the early 60's, the Prince Spaghetti Company in Boston's North End did a marvelous job of marketing and promoting spaghetti while little Anthony Martinetti raced home for dinner. All of us who saw those commercials believed we were morally obliged to dine on Prince (usually served with meatballs and sausage) on Wednesdays.

The Thursday night fare usually centers around any sort of beef dish. Pot roast, hamburgers and all the fixings, meatloaf, or pot pies, you name it; they're delicious. Visit with a New Englander on Thursday. Chances are, you'll relish (pun intended) a delicious beef dinner.

Friday evenings are given over to fish. New Englanders truly love to have the Atlantic as a next door neighbor. And, our neighbor provides such a wonderful smorgasbord from which to choose. Haddock, clams, lobster, snapper and so much more are to be had ... right next door! We whip them up in so many ways, and each is better than the last.

Saturday mornings roll around, and folks from Maine to Connecticut are greeted by the aroma of bacon being served next to a tall stack of pancakes served with New England's own maple syrup. Wash that down with a cup of coffee, and you'll believe you're in heaven. (Come to think of it, you are.)

Beans and franks are served on Saturday nights   ... Boston baked beans, of course. A very large pot is always found bubbling away on stoves from Dover to Montpelier. Oh, and two or three plates per person is traditionally expected by the cook.

I don't know about you, but I'm generally very hungry come supper time. And any supper, any day of the week is fine with me. Bon appetit!

NEW ENGLANDERS HAVE A SENSE OF HUMOR

*So much humor in the Wonderful Six is in the form of "zingers."
We zing everything . . . ethnicity, old folks, young folks, politics
(especially politics), ourselves and sports (Yankees, in particular).*

Some folks think New Englanders don't have a sense of humor. Those folks are from outside the Great Kingdom of the Northeast, and they have us confused with New Yorkers. The possible reason why we New Englanders seem witless is the folks in "The Other 44" can't make humor work as well as we. So many people in other parts of the country may have a funny bone or two, but they want the listener to know where exactly the joke is. Too often, you will hear someone say, "This is a joke." It will be followed by something reasonably witty. It will be then followed by, "That was a joke." Certainly those folks wouldn't want the listener to believe that everything coming out of that person's mouth could possibly be humorous.

So much humor in the Wonderful Six is in the form of "zingers." We zing everything . . . ethnicity, old folks, young folks, politics (especially politics), ourselves and sports (Yankees, in particular).

The truth is, those of us who inhabit this spectacular region can dish it out as well as take it. Hey, haven't there been one or two lines about "The Curse" which plagued the Red Sox for 86 years? But wasn't revenge sweet? And, weren't the one-liners terrific?

"The U.S. Postal Service has decided to put pictures of the Yankees on their stamps. Now people don't know what side to spit on. (That joke was loved by Red Sox Nation and hated by the Evil Empire.)

New Englanders don't like to brag (we do, actually, but its not the socially-correct thing to do); however, we're a fairly intelligent group, and we can manufacture a turn of phrase woven into our communication that is nearly lethal). Certainly, if your side splits open often enough, it has to hurt.) It can be very disarming, if you're not from New England. We use it all . . . oxymoron, pun (very disposable humor, but I love it), exaggeration, understatement, subtle references to Greek mythology . . . everything. You name it, we use it. If you happen to be on the receiving end of a New Englander's verbal machine gun, you can suffer arterial bleeding to your feelings in nothing flat.

We have our patron saints (those who inspire us to explore thin ice and attempt to get away with it). Folks such as Jay Leno, Adam Sandler (born in

New York, but cut his comedy teeth in Manchester, NH, Steve Wright (also born under the flag of the Evil Empire, but whose folks had the wisdom to move to Boston, Dennis Leary (very distant cousin or so my Aunt Helen tells me, and fellow denizen from Main South Worcester), and Paula Poundstone (transplant from Birmingham, Alabama to Sudbury, Massachusetts).

What makes New Englanders wittier than say, someone from Florida or Arizona? Well, the weather is a good bet. Sometimes you just have to laugh at it, or you'll go insane.

"The sun came out this morning, and then I woke up."

It could be the tightness of our ethnic communities or maybe reactions to tragedy.

"Sorry to hear your mom died."

"Yeah, well, she was trying to hold out for another Red Sox World Series win, but she was already 107." (That was a bone for Yankee fans.)

Whatever it is, whatever magic we possess, New Englanders are funny folk . . . and that's no joke.

NEW ENGLAND MUSEUMS

New England does have museums really worth seeing.

I'm a museum kind of guy. If I'm travelling, I love to step inside the doors of a building full of art or artifacts. To me, those places are fascinating. (Here comes the fine print.) I am not, however, enamored by so many roadside museums which dot the landscape in various parts of the country. No offense to the wonderful folks in Kansas (I graduated from college there . . . I love the place. Honest!) but there are far too many of the "Mom and Pop" variety of museums for me.

"This exit – The Great Museum of Nuts and Bolts." You're only 19 miles to The Giant Museum of Small Stuff. Don't Miss it." "Bill's Museum of Blue Things and Buffet" next left." Enough with those places! Somebody get a grant and put all of them under one roof. It would be a fascinating way to spend a half hour.

New England does have museums really worth seeing. From art to natural history, or from New England history to the slightly more unconventional . . . there are some great places far too numerous to mention in this short piece.

In Bennington, Vermont, a definite stop is the Bennington Museum. Everything from "Grandma Moses" art to fine collections of dishware is housed there. If your taste runs to music history, try the Estey Organ Museum in Brattleboro. It's a small place, but it houses a fine collection from the town's organ company. Think you know everything about fun on the slopes? Try the Vermont Ski Museum in Stowe. I bet you'll be amazed. For the best possible museum experience in Vermont, and possibly all of New England, you'll definitely need to experience the Shelburne Museum in the town of the same name. The word "amazing" doesn't even come close to describing the wonders of the place. My favorite attraction is the circus exhibit. It is beyond belief! Go see it, and tell me if I'm wrong.

In Concord, New Hampshire, the Christa McAuliffe Planetarium is a definite must. Named for the state's own teacher in space, the exhibits and presentations are spectacular. The Currier Museum in Manchester was certainly a surprise to me. O'Keefe, Monet, Picasso and so much more are all under one roof. What a treat! The Strawberry Banke Museum in Portsmouth allows the visitor more than 300 years of life in the region. It's a neighborhood.

You'll love it.

If you like trains, you really need to visit the Boothbay Railway Village in Maine. It is an excursion into the railway history of the state. Try it at Christmas time. It's an experience you'll want to sample more than once. And, if you think you can get there from here (old Maine joke), you must experience the Owls Head Transportation Museum. If you want to see how life really was in northern New England, you'll want to stop at the Bangor Museum and Center for History. It houses over 10,000 photographs of life from the last 140 years. My, how the times have changed. If the ocean is your forte, you'll thrive on the exhibits at the Maine Maritime Museum in Bath. It has everything from lobster fishing to ship building, and the storytelling is not to be missed.

You say you have a year or two to kill and you like museums. Hmm, try Massachusetts. Celtics fans (okay, all basketball fans) will enjoy the Basketball Hall of Fame in Springfield. From the invention of the game in 1891 to the exhibits on everything about the game . . . the place is assuredly a basketball feast. Knights from the Medieval era more to your liking. You surely will want to go to the Worcester Art Museum (WAM). You see, the Higgins Armory recently closed its doors, and the WAM inherited all of that magnificent armor. Couples used to get married in the Armory, but I'm not certain if that is still true of the Art Museum (Oh, and no jokes about the old battle axe, please). Pack a lunch and toddle off to the Harvard Museum of Natural History in Cambridge. In all honesty, it will be a day you won't forget.

If you're in Providence, Rhode Island with the kids or grandkids, be certain to visit the Providence Children's Museum. The children's garden is a treat for them and for you. Something more for you? You have to experience the Bristol Train of Artillery. It's crammed with muskets and cannons from the Revolutionary War. You'll get a bang out of the place. (Sorry, couldn't resist.)

Love nostalgia? You'll need to plan a trip to the New England Carousel Museum in Bristol, Connecticut. No, you can't keep the brass ring, but the trip is a definite winner. Take your camera and head to Putney. There, you'll find the Boothe Memorial Park and Museum. If your thing is intricate architecture, it's your kind of place. Take lots of pictures. And, a mere stone's throw from the Foxwoods Casino is the Pequot Museum. To be honest, it is so large and so fascinating, that I have yet to see all of the tremendous regional Native American exhibits the place has to offer.

You have your work cut out for you. Start visiting!

DINERS – A NEW ENGLAND TRADITION

Diners are not just a place to grab some grub and move on; they offer a moment of hospitality in the workaday world.

"More coffee, Irv?"

"You bet, Mary. I'm loaded with wire to get down to Virginia by sunset, and I'm going to be running on java all day."

"Well, we got the best in the east," she says with a smile.

"I know, Mary. That's why I'm here . . . for the coffee and your smile."

She winks, pours and moves down the counter.

Irv sips and sighs.

This scene could be happening at nearly any hour of the day on nearly any day of the week. Diners are not just a place to grab some grub and move on; they offer a moment of hospitality in the workaday world.

Diners are found throughout the country, but they have their roots here in New England. In Providence, Rhode Island in 1858, Walter Scott was a part-time pressman and decided to enhance his income by selling sandwiches out of a basket to newspapermen in men's clubs. By 1872, business was so good that Scott quit his day job and began to sell sandwiches and coffee out of a small horse-drawn wagon on the streets of Providence. His wagon caught on, and soon others were moving similar wagons through other cities in the northeast.

In 1891, Charles Palmer received the first patent for a lunch wagon. In 1901, he built the first "fancy night café" in Worcester, Massachusetts. This was a stationary version of the wagon on wheels. It may have been no accident that it happened in Worcester. The great number of factory workers in the city's great shops provided an instant clientele.

The clientele still finds its way to those great New England diners. They are definitely worth the visit. With any luck, you may run into Irv on his way back from Virginia. He always has great stories to tell, and Mary will be delighted to keep the coffee coming.

THE KINGS OF ICE CREAM

What's the mania today? Why, it's ice cream. Of course!

The town of Waterbury, Vermont lies about midway between Burlington and the beautiful state capitol, Montpelier. It's a quaint little place and well beyond the "sheep mania" of the mid 1800's. What's the mania today? Why, it's ice cream. Of course!

And who began this craze? Ben Cohen and Jerry Greenfield! Not bad for the two slowest, fattest kids in their seventh grade gym class who now bill themselves as the "quintessential '60's hippies," huh?

After college in 1977, they figured that ice cream was their past, present and future. It was their passion. They took a correspondence course on the subject from Penn State and aced it. What did they do about it? Well, they took an abandoned gas station and turned it into their first ice cream shop. And, the rush was on!

You might ask, "What makes Ben and Jerry's ice cream so delicious? (Thanks for asking.) Aside from the fact that they use huge amounts of cream and only true natural ingredients, there is one little secret. There's very little air in it. It is amazingly thick and rich. The main plant packs about 200 pints a minute. And the flavors . . . if they don't have it, you don't want it! They have everything from Cherry Garcia to the Full Vermonty, and from Karamel Sutra to Chunky Monkey.

And, if a batch fails to pass the taste test, what happens then? Why, it goes into the compost pile. The location of that pile, however, is a trade secret.

The containers feature black spots on a white background which look very similar to the contented cows which provided the milk that was turned into the cream that was mixed with the goodies that produced the wonderful concoction known as Ben and Jerry's Ice Cream.

Take a trip to Waterbury. You'll enjoy the place. While you're there, take a tour of the plant. You'll probably like that, too. You can pick up a t-shirt, or a mug, or a postcard, or maybe even a pair of Ben and Jerry socks. You can sample the ice cream if you like (What's not to like?) If you purchase a cone, you can get a free dish of ice cream for your dog. (Proof of dog ownership is required.) On Mother's Day, Mom can get a free dish of ice cream. (Proof of motherhood is required . . . gray hair will do.)

Where can one find Ben and Jerry's Ice Cream? (Another great question.) You can probably find it in your neighborhood grocery store where those other frozen treats are found. If you're lucky, you can track down one of the 430 scoop stores across the country. And, if you find yourself stranded abroad, there are 150 scoop stores around the world, too.

So, what's the best way to fight global warming? (Super question!) Dig into a bowl of Ben and Jerry's Ice Cream. You pick the flavor. They'll supply the taste.

HALLOWEEN IN NEW ENGLAND

It's a chilly time and a chilling time.

No other occasion seems to typify New England as does Halloween. The event just seems tailor-made for this wonderful region as much as this fall classic. Why? Glad you asked.

The weather here is just perfect. By the end of October, summer is a distant memory and fall is just about into its terminal stages. Most of the leaves have fallen and the sky is tending to turn to an inky gray. And, it's cold out there! Many a mom buys a costume for her kid sizes too large so as to accommodate the snowsuit that will go underneath it. It's a chilly time and a chilling time.

The harvest season is complete now. The aroma of freshly-picked apples being turned into a myriad of wonderful items fills the air.

The corn mazes are always a challenge, not so much for the little ones, but we of the gray-haired set require a compass.

And, the big ticket item, the pumpkin is now fair game to be transformed into a jack-o-lantern! It is difficult to pass a front porch or a stone wall and not see at least one orange goblin leering at you with candlelit eyes.

Trick-or-treaters swarm through the streets. Moms and dads are often in close proximity to quickly move the ghosties and gremlins from one house to the next. Empty bags replace filled ones and dentists simply wait in the wings.

For those who choose not to prowl the neighborhoods, parties abound. Schools, churches, youth groups, fraternal organizations . . . virtually everyone have a ghoulish gala for kids or all ages. My particular favorites are the "horror homes." There are some very imaginative but creepy folks out there. Draculas pop out of closets. Skeletons rise up out of staircase hideaways. And, witches abound. There are screams aplenty.

For the more adventurous, there are tours through haunted graveyards. New England has at least one or two very old cemeteries which really lend themselves to a macabre meander. Those creaky old gates and grim tombstone inscriptions are just perfect for the addition of a few dozen white hairs.

A particularly grim but delightful place to visit is Salem, Massachusetts. We're talking Halloween here, folks! They have it all . . . the Festival of the Dead, the Witches Halloween Ball, a psychic fair and so much more. More than one visitor has reported a vision of those poor victims accused of witchcraft so long ago. Revenge is a dish best served up on a cold October night, I guess.

You want horror? I got your horror. Right here . . . the Field of Screams in

West Greenwich, Rhode Island may be just the place for you to shake off our earthly coil. They've got a howling harried and a Psycho House of Horrors to die for. (Sorry, I couldn't resist.)

For the true pumpkin aficionado, Laconia, New Hampshire is the place to go. Keene held the world's record for the most carved squash at the Pumpkin Festival, but it has since moved to the Lakes Region. In recent years, Boston has tried to capture the crown, but it didn't hold a candle to the Keene event.

Oh, there is no truth to the rumor that Stephen King enjoys a giddy and gory night on the town of Halloween. The truth is that he simply enjoys curling up with a good book on this night. Who can blame him? Its just a little too frightening beyond his front door.

OTHERS WHO VISIT
NEW ENGLAND

*... these events aren't from ancient history. Records started be-
ing kept in 1951. So, read on ... if you dare.*

Some folks come from other states to visit New England. Others come from
other countries. Some visitors come from even farther. (Do I hear the theme
from Close Encounters?) Actually, Gentle Reader, I have no feeling on the
subject of alien visitors one way or the other. I can't say I have run into
anyone who doesn't claim earthly residence, but I haven't met everyone yet.
Let me say that people see what they see. Sometimes, what they happen to
see over this fair domain of New England isn't from New England. (Hey, it's
a great place to visit. Right?)

The folks who report seeing what they see aren't necessarily summer
toboggan riders or have nothing better to do with their time. I'm not here
to pass judgment. After all, I'm simply the messenger. The following is not a
complete listing of "sightings." Further, these events aren't from ancient history. Records started being kept in 1951. So, read on ... if you dare.

From New Hampshire: In September 1961, two policemen in Exeter saw
a large dark object with red lights circling a farm and scaring the animals.
I wonder if it had a hole in the center. In 1991, people in North Stratford
saw an object as large as a house glowing with pink and blue lights. A birth
announcement? Maybe. In Hampton from March 17-25, 1998, folks saw a
large green tadpole-shaped object streaking across the sky over the ocean.
Say, wasn't that the same week as college spring break? In Concord in August of 2000, a man and his wife were sitting on the back porch and saw a
bright white light zip across the sky faster than any plane they had ever seen.
Hmm, Lucky Strike maybe?

From Massachusetts: The town of my birth, Worcester, seems to have
cornered the market on UFO sightings. Here's one: On December 28, 1977,
folks saw a large object hovering close to a parking lot. It moved very slowly
and then left. Spaces for those after-Christmas sales are difficult to find. In
Westfield in March of 1962, witnesses saw a red ball jet across the sky. I
thought that the Red Sox didn't play at home until April. In 1989, in Webster,
people saw a large circular object ascend from the lake and disappear. Moon
over Webster?

From Maine: Near Rangeley in 1954, folks saw two white lights descend into a valley and stay there for about 15 minutes. Maybe they just wanted some alone time. On June 28-29, Kennebunk in 1981, a resident saw a large football-shaped object with green and white lights pass over his house and then go out over the ocean. Were the Bushes in town that week? In Bangor in 1963, a resident saw a large white-domed object hovering over the road. He pulled over, yanked out a pistol and shot at it. It took off at a rapid clip. Well, sure. I would, too.

From Vermont: In Goshen, in 2000, witnesses saw a fireball appear in the sky and disappear. I guess the local movie theater had shown everything those folks had seen already. In Jericho in 1999, folks attest to seeing a blue, green and red object dance across the sky. To the tune of what? In Colchester in 1997, a green object was seen jumping about the sky. They also reported their radio was fried for about 10 seconds. Maybe it wasn't jumping. Maybe it was dancing.

From Connecticut: In February of 1999 in New Haven, a person saw a red and blue pulsating object hovering over a neighbor's house. "I see the light. I see the party light . . ." In Old Saybrook in 1957, a woman reported to have seen a UFO with portholes hovering outside her bedroom window. Suggestion: Draw your shades at night, lady! From Woodmount in 1997, residents saw a large saucer-shaped object with a row of windows on the bottom. Tour bus, I bet.

From Rhode Island: In 1998, a person in Portsmouth saw a large amber and gold object pass above some trees. Now that color scheme shows taste. In East Greenwich in 1997, a person saw a cigar-shaped object move across the sky. Churchill or robusto?

Message to all visitors: Try the salt water taffy. It's delicious.

NEW ENGLAND BLUES

(Sung to the tune of Margaritaville)

My tan's turned to snow white.
I think I got frostbite.
Been battling' flu while I shoveled the walk.
Rubbin my hands raw,
Hopin' that they'll thaw.
Coughin' so much, can't breathe when I talk.

Chorus: Wicked cold again in New England, yeah.
Been snowin' here since the Fourth of July.
Weatherman says 'nother storm's comin' in.
And, I think that I'm just goin' to die.

The snow on the roof fell
Way up past the doorbell.
Should've gone south when the birds left in June.
Still sleetin' come Easter.
I froze off my keister.
20 below, and its mid-afternoon.

Chorus: Wicked cold in New England, yeah.
Been snowin' here since the Fourth of July
Airport's closed up now, so is my nose,
And the doc says that I'm just goin' to die.

The car won't thaw out.
Can't seem to get out.
Cabin fever takes over my brain.
But I got the feelin'
They'll find me next season,
Stiff as a post or completely insane.

Chorus: Wicked cold in New England, yeah.
Been snowin' here since the Fourth of July.
My scotch is gone, and the beer's runnin' low.
And I know, I'm just goin' to die.

SURFING NEW ENGLAND

Surfin' safaris from P'town to Popham Beach are nearly as popular as the plethora of tailgate parties at a Patriots' game.

You're standing at high tide a little after sunset at Truro. The waves are beginning to peak. The gulls are screeching as they circle overhead. All that you've read about Cape Cod is true. You've just spent an evening, and you want to stay. You close your eyes and a haunting melody runs though your head. What is it? Of course, "Surfin' USA" (or "Little Surfer," your choice).

That's right. 'Hanging ten' in the Great Northeast is a good deal more popular than I would have ever imagined. Keep in mind, my body is used to 'hangin' two,' that's two hands on the shovel after a nor'easter. The idea of catching the perfect wave off the coast of Sunset Bay or Kennebunkport or Hampton is just a little beyond my realm. I'm either turning into an old Yankee, or just turning old. I can't do it, but I'm all in favor of the crowds who drag their long boards down to the beach, throw on their wet suits, and go out there to play chicken with icebergs.

I've stood by the seawall a little south of Rye, New Hampshire in January. Yes, I stood there and shivered in my thermal head warmer, my insulated gloves, my two sweaters and down-filled coat, my nylon long johns, and my inch-thick woolen socks inside my hunter's all-weather, cold-resistant boots and watched a flock of surfers set sail to shoot the curl. I watched until my teeth chattered and my eyeballs nearly froze in my head. I watched them as the snowflakes nearly obscured them from sight. I watched them as I lumbered back to my car and waited for the engine to warm. I watched them as my icy breath fogged the windshield. Then, I toasted them at home with a very hot Irish coffee in front of a crackling fire in my living room hearth, as I attempted to bring some feeling back into my toes.

When I was a teenager (back at the dawn of time in the early 60's), surfing in New England was in its infancy. Surfers then, were about as plentiful as roses in January. My, how the times have changed! Surfin' safaris from P'town to Popham Beach are nearly as popular as the plethora of tailgate parties at a Patriots' game. (Sorry, sometimes I'm just swept out to sea on a wave of alliteration.)

It bears mentioning that the regional Am-Vets organizations are extremely active in assisting Wounded Warriors to once again enjoy life as they catch the waves of New England. I tip my hat to these marvelous individuals, and I am especially grateful to those who sacrificed life and limb to preserve America's freedom.

The surf shop pros along the coast are the real deal. They cater to true surfers . . . the surfers of New England . . . the hearty breed . . . the gutsy group with blue skin and purple lips. They pride themselves in turning rookie New England wave-walkers into accomplished motion–of-the-ocean Big Kahunas. (Sorry, talking surf just causes me to wax poetic.) Oh, and speaking of wax, those places have gallons of the right stuff to coat your board. Drop in anytime. Those gnarly dudes behind the counters would love to talk surf with you. You may want to drop into a local Dunkin' Donuts and bring them a cup of coffee . . . iced coffee, that is.

THE MAINE COON CAT

*The Maine Coon Cat has tufted ears, wide padded paws,
a huge fluffy tail, bright eyes and lots and lots of fur.
But what makes these cats so remarkable is their size.*

Some professional football teams bear the names of states. A vegetable, a fruit, a tree, and many more items may bear a state name before the actual word. The Minnesota Vikings Georgia peaches and California redwoods come readily to mind. But how many states want to boldly place their names in front of a four-legged, fur-bearing feline? (I apologize. That was intentional alliteration. I won't do it again . . . in this piece.) You guessed it. None! New Englanders are proud to lay claim to that feat with the Maine Coon Cat.

This lovable creature rules over homes and barns from Bar Harbor to Barstow, California. It comes in all the standard fur colors of any other domestic cat. To me, however, it is most striking in brown.

The Maine Coon Cat has tufted ears, wide padded paws, a huge fluffy tail, bright eyes and lots and lots of fur. But what makes these cats so remarkable is their size. Thirteen to eighteen pounds for these critters is not uncommon. There are some supposed myths of Maine Coons topping the scales at over thirty pounds, but I'm not sure those tales can be fully believed.

Once, Child Bride and I were meandering through an antique store in Carson City, Nevada at twilight. When we brought our meager finds to the register for purchase, the bear skin rug, which seemed to be draped over the counter, stood. Its piercing yellow eyes caught the fading sunlight, and it seemed to gaze into my soul (or at least into my wallet). The cat was huge! It leaned off the counter and butted its head into mine. "Don't worry," said the store owner. "He's a Maine and he's really friendly . . . most times." The cat merely looked into my eyes and winked.

One history of the cat includes a tall tale that it originated from a love affair between a raccoon and a Maine house cat. That didn't happen. Another tale is that Marie Antoinette was on her way to Maine to escape the guillotine and sent six of her fluffy pets here before her. There's possibly no truth to that one either. More than likely, the Vikings had a few cats on those long ships, and when they hopped out onto New England's rocky shore, their four-legged raiders did also. Those cats probably did their share of pillaging while cavorting with the local short hairs. The result was a cat that is perfectly adapted for the intense New England winters.

Maine Coons don't meow, but they do have a deep purr that sounds like a motorboat idling. In addition, they make a solid thud when they jump from the bed. They're not really lap cats, but they will follow you from room to room . . . probably to see what's for lunch.

Two Maine Coons rule our home. Named No-No and Ya-Ya, they probably should have been knighted Catastrophe and Catatonic. By day, they catch z's at any soft, warm place they can find. They prowl by night and are frequently seen looking out the window in the direction of the shore. My guess is that they're wondering when the next Viking ship is due back.

THE WONDERFUL WORLD OF READING

Ah, New England . . . a crackling fire in the hearth . . .
soft music on the radio . . . and, a good book.

To New Englanders, reading is not just a pastime; it is a passion. It's not just an occasion to keep one from a rabid case of cabin fever during an interminably frigid winter, or something to occupy one's moments between people-watching while at the beach. Folks in the Great Six actually enjoy reading on just about any and all occasions.

Youngsters in this region end a school year with their reading lists in hand. They whoop at the fact that they don't have to see "ol' what's-his-name" or "what's her face" ever again and immediately trudge off to the local library to stock up on the required tomes before all the next graders do. Amazingly, they are as religious about reading as they are about the Red Sox.

"Hey, didya hear the game last night?"

"Yeah! Wow! Wasn't Manny terrific? Four for four at the plate, and that pick-off play at second!'

"Yeah, the Sox are like Ahab and Moby is the Yankees."

"No way, man, Moby's cool. The Yankees just get paid big bucks and choke."

New England teens are just as hormonal as their peers in the rest of the country. They're just better read. Friday night is still date night from Bangor to Boston, but young adults frequent bookstores and libraries with as much regularity as they do the video store or the pizza parlor. Besides, they're great places to scope out members of the opposite sex.

"Dude, check out that girl with the armload of fiction heading this way.' (She must have just received her summer reading list.)

"For real, man. Awwright! King! My kind of girl!'

There should be a statue of Park Benjamin in every city and town in the northeast. As you will recall, it was Benjamin, who, in 1840, published the first paperback novel, Charles O'Malley. He was hoping to sell 10,000 copies to prove to investors that there was interest. He proved it. He sold 25,000!

New Englanders can be seen with the latest best-seller or a true classic poking out of their hip pockets while carrying groceries, or neatly placed atop their laptops while taking the 5:15 home from work. Reading . . . it's what we do. It's who we are.

For the record, Kindles are now the rage. I'm an old dog, however, and that's a new trick.

Every occasion is an occasion to read. If a wedding or a funeral becomes boring, many folks in the Northeast simply whip out the latest Ludlum or Coontz, and they're perfectly comfortable.

Drivers in New England are used to traffic jams. Some even look forward to them. They simply wait for the rush on the interstate to grind to a halt, reach over to the passenger seat, snag the book in which they are currently ensconced and await the gentle, melodious honk from the driver behind them to signify the resumption of moving traffic.

While driving up one of Worcester's seven hills, a sudden frost iced the snow melt-off, which had begun to stream across the road. Traffic snarled, and I grabbed my Robert E. Howard. Moments later, a strange motion to my left caught my attention. The car headed downhill started to slide across the road directly at me. I rolled my window down as I watched the phenomenon. All the way across, the driver of the other car was apologizing about the impending crash. After several seconds, we were door handle to door handle.

"I'm so sorry. The car was out of my control. I couldn't help it," he said sincerely. Then, he glanced into my hands. "Hey, Howard, I love Howard, but I'm a Burroughs man."

We had a great conversation. I now own the entire Burroughs collection.

There is a downside to reading. On numerous occasions, I have lugged a great book to the dinner table. Child Bride is a wonderful woman, but she won't play second fiddle to Patterson or Puzo. So, I pay her all of the attention that is her due and race through my meal to hurry back to my book. An hour or so later, I can't remember if I ate. Worse yet, I can't remember what it was! This definitely does not make for the most endearing after-dinner conversations.

Ah, New England . . . a crackling fire in the hearth . . . soft music on the radio . . . and, a good book. I wonder if Child Bride is home. I wonder if there are any leftovers from dinner.

LAND OF PRESIDENTS

I would like to point out a few of our nation's leaders
just happened to hail from the great northeast.

Are New Englanders politically active? Only about as much as it may snow in Maine during the winter. Oh, yes, the folks from the great northeast get involved. Lest you forgot, that little incident involving some tea and the birth of a new nation happened somewhere around here. New Hampshire just happens to be the first state to cast its ballots in each primary election. If you really want to be first, you should live in Dixville Notch; it is the first community in the state to vote! And, just because I'm a little fond of the place, I would like to point out a few of our nation's leaders just happened to hail from the great northeast.

Now, I hate baseball stats with asterisks. It usually means that the player, team, or game didn't really merit being considered in this category because . . ..These arguments can go on ad nauseam, and the final answer is, "So what?" Well, a few asterisks are about to show up. All they mean is that the names they follow became presidents before this country became a bonafide nation. Got a problem with that? No? Good!

Chester Arthur and Calvin Coolidge were born in Vermont. George W. Bush came into this world in Connecticut. His dad, George Bush, John Adams* John Quincy Adams*, and John Kennedy all called Massachusetts their birth state. New Hampshire was the birthplace of Franklin Pierce.

If you're doing the math, and not the historical geography, you'll see that eight presidents came from the region. That's nearly 19% of the nation's presidents!

These are some diversified men. Some controversial. Some dynamic. All of them hold some place of recognition in this nation's history. All of the men held their religious beliefs; those, too, were diversified.

John F. Kennedy was Roman Catholic. Calvin Coolidge was a Congregationalist. Chester Arthur, Franklin Pierce and George Bush were Episcopalians. George W. Bush was a Methodist. John Adams and John Quincy Adams were Unitarians.

New England's presidents did more than hold the seat in the Oval Office. Many were military men as well. Some were heroes. All were willing to die to keep America free.

Franklin Pierce served in the Mexican War. George Bush and John

Kennedy served in World War II. George W. Bush was in the military but saw no action.

None of our presidents was born into the office. Each had a career prior to taking the oath of office.

John Adams, John Quincy Adams, Calvin Coolidge, Franklin Pierce and Chester Arthur were lawyers. George Bush and George W. Bush were oilmen. John Kennedy was a journalist. Chester Arthur and Franklin Pierce were school teachers.

Some of these men had facial hair. Most didn't. Some of these men had problems with alcohol. Most didn't. Some of these men had extramarital affairs. Most didn't. One even slept ten hours a day. The point of these lists is not to determine which New England president was the best. That debate would be nearly endless. Simply, the point is that men (sorry, no women as of yet) have served the nation in the highest office of the land. Some of their differences have been noted. Most have not.

If one thing can be said for New England, it is a land of uniqueness. The contradiction in that uniqueness is the diversity of its people. Certainly these presidents form a varied collection of leaders. They represented New England. They led the nation.

THE RIGHT TIME FOR ICE CREAM

*Amigo's Ice Cream Store. Their special this month
is triple-double chocolate surprise.*

New Englanders give the best directions to visitors in the region. If you pull over to ask anyone hiking, riding their bike or walking their dog, they will most certainly tell you how to get from here to there.

"Excuse me, could you tell me how to get to the Spendmore Antique Shop?"

"Sure thing, pahdner. You turn right up there at Amigo's Ice Cream Store. Their special this month is triple-double chocolate surprise. You go about two miles past the Contented Cows Dairy. Oh, they have the best plum swirl delight. You go two miles to the Yankee Ice Cream Dairy. That's the home of 160 flavors of homemade ice cream . . . and, it's right across the street from the Spendmore Antique Shop. But, you probably won't arrive as thin as you were when you left this house."

Almost everyone will agree that New Englanders are a hardy lot, especially New Yorkers. We bask in the glory of storms past; cold spells to rival Siberia; humidity so thick that arm movement causes rain; and rain in such torrents that we sometimes feel the need to break out an ark.

Whether it's the climate or the hardy stock, New Englanders do love their ice cream. Summer, fall, winter and spring . . . we're ready for a double scoop of choca-mocha nut crunch with jimmies, please.

The average American eats about 48 pints of ice cream a year, far more than any other country on the planet. New Englanders leave the rest of the country way back in hot fudge. We are the number one ice cream consuming region from border to border. Depending on whose figures you use, New Englanders eat anywhere from 51-86% more ice cream than the rest of the nation! We're talking gallons more per person.

A drive through the countryside is virtually not complete without a stop at the local ice cream store or dairy. (The dairies, however, are generally a summertime thrill.) Perhaps the cows are not exactly enamored by their position on the ice cream food chain. A would-be ice cream eater is very likely to come across a line of cars on the side of the road and a stern-faced policeman there to keep order. Once, as I inched my way up to a guardian of law and order, I rolled down my window.

"What's the problem up ahead," I asked.

He swaggered over to the side of my vehicle, doffed his hat, and took on a very concerned appearance. This man was no one with whom I wanted to trifle.

"They're out of peanut splash and blueberry moose. It looks as though strawberry jazz and caramel cluster are in serious jeopardy."

"Dang," I mumbled. "And, it had been such a beautiful day."

Ah, but there's nothing like a hot fudge sundae to warm a heart on a cold winter's night. Just recently I came in after shoveling and reshoveling, and once again for good measure, to find Child Bride at the dinner table just waiting for me to put aside my shovel and take up my spoon. Yes, that woman really loves me.

My best friend's mom was terrific. Once, I called him, and she invited me over.

"He'll be home soon, but I was just cleaning out the freezer. I need to make room. There are about five gallons of ice cream in here, and I've got to get rid of it."

"I'll be right over," I said. And, I was.

After an hour or so of devouring the delicious treats, my friend would arrive with a couple of large bags tucked under his arm.

"What do you have there," I would ask.

"Three gallons of ice cream," he would say. "You're going to have some, aren't you?"

I stayed, of course. Hey, what are friends for?

SHOPPING THE ARCADE

The American adventure in malls began in Providence,
Rhode Island in 1828. The Arcade was, and still is,
an elegant shopping experience.

"Mom, like Mary and Grace are like comin' over, and like we're goin' to the mall. And, like Tommy and Chuck will be there . . . but, like I don't want to see Chuck. He took out his nose ring and cut his hair. Like, ugh! Like, he looks so geeky now. And, like there's a new Z-Pop Video store . . . and like a new railing in front of Le Phone Shoppe . . . and, like there are new tables in the food court."

"That's nice, dear, but what are you going to buy?"

"Like . . . buy?"

Malls seem to be the new Mecca drawing young adults to the hip world of what is considered to be the latest and greatest in the worlds of fashion, technology and entertainment. Malls, however, didn't just spring into existence since the advent of the Ipod. They've been in existence for quite some time. The Great Bazaar in Tehran dates back to the 10th century A.D.

The American adventure in malls began in Providence, Rhode Island in 1828. The Arcade was, and still is, an elegant shopping experience. Done in Greek Revival style, the building features a great bakery and charming restaurants. A large window in the ceiling provides ample natural lighting, while the stone columns, decorative ironwork, and use of highly polished woods reminds shoppers of an elegant, less hurried time.

The Arcade is a three-story establishment and might be considered to be the anchor building in downtown Providence. Yet, even though it was built at a time when whaling was the premier business in New England, the Arcade very closely resembles a Greek temple. It took many teams of oxen to drag the heavy granite columns to the site from a quarry in Johnston.

During World War II, the Arcade came close to shutting its doors for good. Since then, it has survived the tough financial times of the '70's and '80's. It has been refurbished and is attracting large crowds daily. One of the main features of the Arcade is the vast space for exhibits and special events. The Arcade has some 35 specialty shops and is wheelchair accessible and smoke free, but, sorry, folks, there are no pets allowed.

The Arcade, along with the Rhode Island Black Heritage Society Museum on the third floor, is located on the Banner Trail of cultural and historical attractions in Providence. Certainly, it is just one more reason to enjoy a leisurely constitutional through one of New England's great cities.

So, like go to the Arcade. Tommy, and, like, ugh, Chuck will be there. Oh, and you don't have to wear your nose ring!

RED SOX NATION

Yes, Red Sox Nation is New England,
but it goes beyond our borders.

As a boy, when summer rolled around, I used to walk down the sidewalk and listen to the Red Sox games on the radio. Not my radio. Every radio on the street! Every house on the block would have the Sox on, and I never missed a pitch. On more than one occasion, I would stop in front of a house to listen to a particularly thrilling play. I didn't want to miss any of the action in the ten to twenty feet of "fuzz one" between radios.

Then, along came television, and the magic of the game on the airwaves disappeared with the black and white image on the screen. That was fine with me. I had the voice of Curt Gowdy to take me through the summers. Ah, did he love to talk baseball.

When I was twelve, I was hit with an appendicitis attack. I had to spend a week in a semi-private room with an elderly gentleman who didn't say much. He seemed to have a passion for only two things: reading and the Red Sox. Each day at game time, he would lay the book on the night stand and flip on the television to the Sox. He was involved in every pitch of every game. The Sox went on a terrific home stand; it was enough to send him home with a smile and nine completed books.

I remember going to my first game somewhere back about the dawn of time. I was with three or four guys from our Boy Scout troop. We had bleacher seats. They probably cost about a buck or two, but they were terrific. We sat in straightaway center and we munched pizza and drank Coke all afternoon. One of the guys snagged an enemy homerun, but that was just fine. The Sox won anyway.

Over the years, and over the miles, I never lost track of the Sox. They were my link to my boyhood . . . my link to New England. Whenever I could, I would catch them on the tube or on radio. Whether I was in college or working in some city across the country, if a game was on, I was there. I never ever missed the morning paper wherever I lived. Therefore, I never missed the box score or any article dealing with "my guys."

When Red Sox Nation became country unto itself, I was teaching in Las Vegas. Now, the beauty of being in Las Vegas is that there are plenty of casinos. Casinos have sports books. Sports books have televisions, and televisions play baseball games . . . all the games. It was like being home again. I would troop on down to the closest casino, purchase a scotch rocks, and take up residence at one of the hundreds of little screens so generously provided for my viewing entertainment. And, entertain me, they did!

In 2004, I was one year away from retirement, and the Sox were poised to make the biggest sensation in baseball history. After an 86-year drought, they came back after being down 3-0 to the Yankees. THEY TOOK THE NEXT FOUR! They went on to sweep the Cardinals in four, and I was a basket case. So was just about everyone in New England, or who had roots here.

In 2014, one of my nieces was graduating from high school. An outdoor part y was given in her honor. At a table off by themselves, sat four of my ancient Italian aunts. I strolled over to say 'hello'. I found myself being soundly shushed for my troubles. They were, of course, listening to the Sox on a radio.

"Hey! Watasamatter for you, eh? Essa da Sox. Go away. Eat a meatball. Leave us alone!"

Point taken.

Yes, Red Sox Nation is New England, but it goes beyond our borders. There are Sox ex-patriots all over the country. They swarm ballparks in both leagues whenever the guys from Beantown are there. They hoist banners. They wear the shirts. They wear "B" caps. They support their team . . . the Boston Red Sox.

Me, I'm a proud member of the Nation. I root for the Sox . . . and any team who beats the Yankees!

ANOTHER VISITOR
TO THE NEW WORLD

In 1873, several railroad workers reported seeing an
"enormous serpent" raise its head out of the water.

Actually, that title is a bit in error. The visitor about whom I speak was most likely here long before any of us ever arrived on the planet. I guess that would make us the visitors. Then again, we're not sure this character even exists. So, that would make us humans the first real visitors. But if he exists . . . I know, I know, "Let it go and tell the story! Okay!"

New England's westernmost border is Lake Champlain. It separates us from pinstripes. The lake was most likely formed some 10,000 years ago when the glaciers were heading back north. The lake is not tiny by any standards. It is over 100 miles long and over 400 feet deep in some places. The place is certainly big enough to house more than a couple of monsters (not to mention a few mothers-in-law).

In 1873, several railroad workers reported seeing an "enormous serpent" raise its head out of the water. Later that year, a tourist boat supposedly hit the creature nearly sending everyone onboard into the lake. Over the next century plus, the sightings of Champ (or "Champie," take your pick) have been continuous.

In 1977, the stories of Champ became more than just a New England legend. Joseph W. Zarzynski, founder of the Lake Champlain Investigation took a snapshot of the critter. Whether or not the picture is real is the subject of much conjecture. A number of expeditions have set out to find any trace of the long-necked wonder. So far, Champ is a no-show.

The study of Champ, and other creatures of that ilk, come under the heading of cryptozoology. Even The word gives you icy shivers, doesn't it?) In essence, it means the study of secretive things. I guess a critter that has been hanging around for several millenniums and has made only a few guest appearances could be described as secretive. Who knows . . . maybe snobbish? Maybe, just maybe, Champ is from the New York side of the lake.

Gentle Reader, New England doesn't need a roadside attraction to boost tourism. The maple trees do quite well for themselves, thank you very much. Further, the folks of Vermont didn't meet in some large grange hall in an attempt to besmirch the reputation of Nessie in Loch Ness, Scotland. For all I know, the Champ and Nessie may get together on weekends with Bigfoot and the Yeti for a game of whist and a few highballs. The claims are documented. The photographs have been examined. The lake is waiting. Go take a look for yourself. Oh, and don't forget to send me a couple of autographed 9x12" glossies!

Michael F. Bisceglia, Jr.

THE SNOWMAN –
NEW ENGLAND ROOTS

*The debate rages on, but most scholars do agree that
the snowman originated in New England.*

There are no artifacts . . . no written records . . . no genealogy. It's a sad commentary of someone who is remembered annually during the winter months. The debate rages on, but most scholars do agree that the snowman originated in New England.

Oh yes, there were crude attempts to build snowmen in Europe, particularly in England during the late 14th and early 15th centuries, but they appeared to be gothic in design and somber in attitude. They resembled cathedrals more than persons of mirth.

Currier, of Currier and Ives fame, was born in Roxbury, Massachusetts. And, although he isn't credited with rolling the first snow ball, he and Ives (who hailed from New York, but we won't talk about him) did depict snowmen standing sentry by ponds, waiting outside front doors, or watching children sled down a hill.

Norman Rockwell, of Stockbridge, Massachusetts, must have been influenced by Currier and the many masons of snowmen in the region. He depicted snowmen in many of his winter scenes.

Snowmen of New England have obviously become health conscious in recent years. Oh, yes, many traditional men in white are composed of the three round balls: base, torso and head. Many, however, have been trimmed down and have sprouted arms and legs. They're also doing more than just standing and holding a broom or merely gawking at passing motorists. Snowmen are now posed as runners, skiers, dog walkers (complete with their own snow dogs), or tree climbers to mention a few.

Snowmen of New England are also very intellectual. Each winter, a myriad of frosty fellows can be found on high school and college campuses from Orono, Maine to Hartford, Connecticut. Some of the seasonal folks found there, male and female alike, are actually anatomically correct, but these are the more free-spirited variety. They have obviously not joined the work force yet.

The guys in white (although as many are now going undercover in numerous other hues) are also found in many of New England's urban centers.

Large numbers have been found in the early morning hours after a snow-storm blocking a street, although what they might be protesting is not exactly clear.

The ability to create snowmen brings out the Frankenstein in some of us. One Live-Free-Or-Dier conscripted a small army just off of his back porch. He had the snowmen poised to leap the wall into his neighbor's yard, and then the sun came out.

Another fellow from the White Mountain region fairly scared the wits out of the young lady who lived next door to him (you will notice the past tense here). He posed one snowman standing atop the shoulders of another peering over the stockade fence into her yard. This probably wouldn't have been such an evil stunt, except he employed 21st century technology. Instead of lumps of coals for eyes, he employed thin green laser lights. The word is that her screams can still be heard echoing down canyon walls.

Other states can have snow angels, snow forts, and twelve-foot tall snow-balls. New England has these, but we also have magnificent snowmen . . . and snowwomen. They come in all sizes and shapes, and they're on duty from early November until early May . . . sometimes later.

ONCE A NEW ENGLANDER, ALWAYS A NEW ENGLANDER

Yes, New England is my home. I appreciate it. I love it, and I'm delighted it has welcomed me home again.

Although New Englanders are from God's country, we sometimes (but not often) make mistakes. The foremost cardinal error is leaving the region. No one is ever banished. Some of us, however, think that life would be so much better somewhere else. Let me save anyone who reads this the trouble of taking that test run . . . Don't!

As a young man, I believed that New England was a great place to be from and that life was going to be so much better somewhere else. I packed up the family and started off in search of something better. My rationale was simple, "If life was good here, it had to be so much better somewhere else in the country."

The first stop on my pilgrim was the Midwest. It was a positive experience but didn't hold the magic for me that the Great Six do. Now, there is nothing wrong with flat land. Parking lots are great on wide, flat pieces of earth. Treeless areas are very nice, too. Certainly to build one's home, that piece of land has to be devoid of trees. I found, however, that when large flat areas are combined with a treeless existence, feelings of being stranded set in. The people were warm, but the topography was just too vast. There seemed to be just miles and miles of miles and miles.

The South was my next destination. There's a lot to be said that is positive about the south, but I found the spoken word just a little too slow and difficult to follow. (On the other hand, I never had to repeat so many things in my life. Most everyone I met believed I had a severe speech impediment.) The weather is great in the southern tier, but you have to love heat and humidity. I'm used to making occasional hand gestures when I speak. Incredibly, when I would move my hands rapidly, it would rain.

California and the territories of the northwest were supposed to be spectacular. They are. They carry with them a price tag and an attitude. I certainly could never afford the price tag, and I never could develop the California attitude. "Valley talk" is not a form of communication easily mastered. Everything appears to be "like" something else, but nothing "is" what it "is." Are you a little lost? So was I.

The Reno – Las Vegas area was next on my shopping list. I had done the research. The price tags were reasonable. Snow came occasionally and disappeared quickly. And all those buffets . . . Oh boy! The catch was that one has to love living in a sand-covered oven to appreciate that environment. Yes, it's a dry heat, but there's so much of it. The center of community life is everything that happens in a casino. That's the bad news. The good news is that those places are severely air conditioned. There is nore bad news . . . you have to plan a several hundred mile excursion to find a tree or a puddle, which on the map is labeled "lake." I know lakes, and those little things don't measure up.

I came back. My children are grown, and my hair is gray, but I came back. Amazingly, my New England dialect is returning without having to take a refresher course. More to my amazement, the Atlantic is still as beautiful and invigorating as it was when I left. The trees are just as green and plentiful now as then. The mountains are still as picturesque. The people are still warm and genuine. Yes, New England is my home. I appreciate it. I love it, and I'm delighted it has welcomed me home again.

THE APPLES ARE RIPE
AND BEGINNING TO FALL!

New England's apples are the best. There are at least
nineteen different varieties of the fruit in the region.

One of the absolute best reasons to visit New England in the fall (aside from the fact that beach tourists are gone) is that the apples are ripe. And, if one has the urge for indulging in sensual delights, there's no place better to be. From mid-August through mid-October, those of us from the resplendent Northeast (and those who are privileged to visit here) flock to the farms.

Upon arrival, you are nearly overwhelmed by the crisp sweetness of the air, because right behind those long, meandering stonewalls is a feast just waiting to be enjoyed. New England's apples are the best. There are at least nineteen different varieties of the fruit in the region. Those in the northern regions tend to ripen early in the season, while the fruit in the southern orchards ripen later. In any case, you may wish to come back again and again to load up on your particular favorites.

The Pippin is my choice. Some may not think that it's the prettiest fruit in the world, but beauty is only skin deep. It is green with yellow highlights, and some may grow to the size of small pumpkins. It's tart (perfect for my personality) and simply a meal all by itself. Cut up a few for a pie or some strudel, and you'll have yourself a banquet.

Speaking of banquets, the orchards not only produce apples; they also grow pears, cherries, nectarines, plums, pumpkins and more. You'll want to leave a lot of space in your trunk when you make your visits. Besides the fruits, many of the farms have shelves of candies, jams and so much more.

One of the greatest treats in visiting (or, if you're lucky) living in New England is that many of the orchards allow you to pick your own fruit. Not only do you have a country moment to savor a great fruit, but no orchard has a dismal view. Let the kids roam a bit, while you treat your eyes to the beautiful vistas the greatest region in the country has to offer.

When the snow flies, you'll want to come out of hibernation to take a sleigh ride across the frozen expanses of some orchards. The ride, a glass of hot apple cider, some oven-fresh cider donuts and a bag of apples that you picked yourself make the visit truly worthwhile.

Hey, if you feel like taking in a movie or reading a good book, you might latch onto The Cider House Rules. It was written by John Irving, who learned a great deal about apples and apple orchards by working at Applecrest Farm in Hampton Falls, NH. Oh, and a few little tidbits about Applecrest that never cease to bring a smile to my face . . . the local high school's theatrical classes perform storybook tales at various crossroads throughout the orchard during the harvest season. In addition, one can savor the full orchard in all of its fall and winter majesty by taking a hayride during the leaf season and a sleigh ride when the snow falls.

John "Johnny Appleseed" Chapman from Leominster, Massachusetts may be considered the Apostle of Apples for planting the seeds for this delicious fruit from New York to Illinois. He was a gentleman with gentle ways, and he certainly gave a tremendous gift that keeps on giving to apple lovers across the country. In no way, however, could he have given America a true appreciation for New England Orchards. You have to be here to really believe how wonderful they are.

Michael F. Bisceglia, Jr.

THE ISLANDS OF NEW ENGLAND

To those visitors from Europe, the islands of
the great northeast are the first points of invitation and
the last places of remembrance.

New Englanders love the waters of the region. Five of the six states border the Atlantic Ocean, and one borders Lake Champlain. Each state has wonderful rivers, picturesque lakes and breathtaking reservoirs. Throw in the ponds, streams and brooks, and we have a geographic region swimming in water . . . okay, bad pun, but folks here do love their water. Not only do we love to fish in it; boat in it; skate on it; drink it and bathe in it, we love to live as close to it as possible. In this fast-paced world, our bodies of water offer us a sense of tranquility as well as a true bond with nature. That's why water-view property is always at a premium.

Folks here don't stop at the water's edge when it comes to enjoying our territory; we have a particular fondness for those little parcels of land which sprout up from the water as well. We hike them, photograph them, pick blueberries on them, paint them and we live there, too. To those visitors from Europe, the islands of the great northeast are the first points of invitation and the last places of remembrance. They are our territories beyond our territory. They are New England.

There are 27 named islands in Connecticut, most of which are located in Fairfield County. "Rough-hewn" may be the only way to describe many of the islands there. Giant granite boulders form the foundations for solid homes only a few yards away from the shoreline. The Thimble Islands, about halfway up the coast from New York to Massachusetts, offer it all. From kayaking to excuses to use up hundreds of rolls of film, this truly is a place to experience. Oh, if you should happen to run across Captain Kidd's treasures as you explore the rocky coastlines, be sure to give me a call.

Rhode Island has about half of the named islands as Connecticut, but one place every hearty visitor must explore is Block Island. It is a rugged locale, but it is nonetheless named the "Bermuda of the North." If you happen to tire from hiking the trails; fishing from the rocks; or simply birdwatching, you may want to catch the Arts Festival in August. You won't be sorry you did.

New Englanders love the west coast . . . the west coast of Vermont, that is. There are only a handful of islands in Lake Champlain, but the beauty of those little patches of land is superb. Yes, the experience is a little too rustic for some people's taste, but Vermont does rural very well. So, okay, you're on South Hero Island. There is a spectacular sunset and you want to offer a toast. What do you do? Why, you go down to the Snow Farm Vineyard and purchase some of their award-winning chardonnay. It goes particularly well with a Vermont sunset.

Let's talk about the islands off the coast of Massachusetts . . . Martha's Vineyard and Nantucket. They are probably the places everyone thinks of when they think New England vacation. They have great shops, views, hikes, restaurants . . . heck, they're just plan great. It gets a tad cool there at night, so don't forget your sweater. You don't want your teeth chattering if you happen to run into a Hollywood celeb or a president, do you?

New Hampshire has only 17 miles of coastline, but it does have some picturesque islands. If you're a history buff, you certainly don't want to miss New Castle Island. Besides the tours of the lighthouses, you can learn all you want to know about the site of America's first naval engagement during the Revolutionary War. The term "New England" was penned by John Smith (remember that little escapade with Pocahontas?) Well, John, among other things developed a fishing colony on the Isles of Shoals. They are about within shouting distance of Hampton Beach, and well-worth the short excursion. Of the five Isles, my favorite is Smuttynose. The name just cracks me up.

Okay, you think you've covered New England from stem to stern? Not quite. There's one more state to consider. The northeastern-most piece of land, just of the coast of Lubec, Maine is Moose Island. (A little controversy here, some folks think its Canadian property.) Bring your binoculars; you certainly don't want to miss out on a whale or two as they swim by. You'll definitely want to see the lighthouses, but you'll want to pick a sunny day to do it. The weather can get downright nasty in these parts. Finally, you may want to plan your trip here around the Fourth of July. The American flag is flown here is the first in the nation to be hoisted that day. Okay, pop quiz! Maine has 3,166 islands. Name 'em!

Welcome to the islands. Enjoy your stay!

FLEA MARKETING –
NEW ENGLAND STYLE

*There just aren't too many places where a couple can go togeth-
er, split up for eight hours, come home with a moose head and
a set of chipped china, and chalk up that day as a success.*

If it is true that one man's junk is another man's treasure, then New England could very well be Fort Knox. It is the ideal place to become an eclectic collector. There just aren't too many places where a couple can go together, split up for eight hours, come home with a moose head and a set of chipped china, and chalk up that day as a success.

In all honesty, flea markets didn't begin in the exceptionally great northeast. That claim to fame probably goes to France during the 1860's. Outdoor bazaars were held, and it was quite common to purchase a piece of furniture that was infested with little critters that bite. Ah, quel domage!

The American version is generally sans the critters. There are about 5,000 such events held within our borders annually, and a great number of them occur where folks call 'em 'flea mahkits.'

There are some notable ones in the region. (It is important to note that these are simply my choices often because of the amenities, not because of the merchandise.) In Maine, the anxious "flea-er" may wish to peruse the goods in the Waterfront Flea market in Brunswick. This place offers a great view of the harbor area, AND it has restrooms (always a plus in my book). The food is good and the prices are reasonable.

Chichester is located in mid-New Hampshire and boasts the A-Town Flea Market. They've got it all in Chichester . . . outdoor and indoor booths (and those booths have electricity, great parking, and they even have a camping area with all the needed facilities).

The Waterbury Flea market, in Vermont, puts on a wonderful flea market each weekend from may through October. It's got everything from antiques to new stuff. If you need a maple snack to curb your sugar desire, you don't want to miss this one.

If you enjoy a great cup of coffee and feel that you don't see enough of your neighbors, you may want to tote along a Dunkin sipper as you amble through the more-than-ample number of tables at Todd's Farm in Rowley, Massachusetts. It's easy enough to find, just ask your neighbors!

The Kiwanis Big K flea Market in Newington, Connecticut has been in existence since 1992. All of the funds raised go to civic and educational projects. It's open on weekends from April through October. The parking is great, and, yes, the restrooms aren't bad either.

The Bi Top Flea market in Providence, Rhode Island is one you may not want to miss. There are 120 venders, new and used merchandise, a super shack bar, and spiffy facilities. It's an indoor market, so don't worry about the elements.

I've been saving the best for last. The Brimfield Fair in Brimfield, MA might be considered the granddaddy of all flea markets. It has been around since the '70's. It is held three times a year on ten fields and boasts some 5,000 dealers with some spectacular deals on their goods, both new and used, collectibles and antiques. In fact, the market is so vast, you may want to pick up a guide book so you can find out what is where. The layout is wonderful; you won't find yourself falling over a rocking chair next to a lamp booth. Did I say they have it all? You bet, and then some. If they don't have it, you don't want it! Suggestion here: the place is so vast, you may want to spread your visit over a couple of days. There is dining on hand and plenty to see and do in the area. The children will definitely be entertained because there is enough silly stuff on hand to placate even the most tired toddler and cranky crone alike.

Flea markets should not be the only reason to come to New England, but they certainly are a good one. One word of advice, make sure you've left a lot of room in your trunk; you certainly won't leave empty-handed.

STONEWALLS AMONG US

These walls were functional, not necessarily decorative. Having esthetically pleasing walls was not an 18th century concept.

There is probably nothing more indicative of New England than its' stonewalls. Constructed primarily of granite (after all, this is the "Granite State"), the walls meander along property lines, through woodlands and around many orchards and cemeteries. So popular were the walls in the late 19th century, that in the New York-New England area, folks erected thousands upon thousands of miles of them.

New Hampshire Yankees were a self-reliant lot. Many needed to grow their own crops and raise their own sheep and livestock. In order to till the land, the large crop of boulders (dropped off courtesy of an Ice Age glacier) had to be moved to the perimeter of the property. It was there that the hefty chunks of stone were placed in a somewhat orderly manner. These walls were functional, not necessarily decorative. Having esthetically pleasing walls was not an 18th century concept. Walls built nowadays around lovely gardens and trimmed lawns might well be considered Victorian in design.

Walls around the many one-acre farms which dotted the area were not tall enough to keep a wayward sheep from bounding into a neighbor's pastureland. Thus, individuals in the area erected wood-framed obstacles on the walls, or simply piled brush atop the stones.

As walls became more standardized, builders took pride in building stonewalls long and straight. Some historians today can tell which walls were built by the same builder.

Since there is considerable marshland in the Hampton area, the number of stonewalls is far fewer than further inland in more hilly terrain. Around both the Pine Grove and Ring Swamp Cemeteries, there are fine stone walls. Interestingly, the walls around the burial sites were added over one hundred years after the cemeteries were realized.

Along the Exeter Road, there are some wonderful stonewalls. At least two of these walls connect the foundations of some early structures. It is true testimony to the builders that these walls remain intact today.

Many of the walls are single stone width. These are only a few feet in height. The double width stonewalls may be a bit higher. Essentially, the double thickness walls are two separate walls with a space in between. The space is filled with smaller stones.

Kevin Gardner's book, *The Granite Kiss* is a wonderful source for anyone seeking information about the picturesque stonewalls of New England. For the uninitiated, the kiss is that exquisite moment in the course of building or repairing a wall when one's fingers become slammed between two unyielding granite stones.

In 1914, Robert Frost wrote the poem, "Mending Wall." In it, two land owners chose a day in spring to walk the length of the wall together. They work together, although it may be considered a form of competition to re-build the wall to separate an orchard from an animal enclosure. Twice in the course of the poem, Frost points to the rugged, practical nature of New Englanders with the line, "Good fences make good neighbors." If this is true, the Hampton area has to have a tremendous amount of good neighbors.

There is beauty in stonewalls, no matter the height, depth or length. Stonewalls, like people, are not perfect. It might be said that their perfection is in their imperfections. An old proverb states, "Gifts make their way through stonewalls." Anyone who walks or bikes along the Northeast's many miles of stonewalls, might disagree. They might just say, "Gifts don't make their way through the walls; they are the walls."

A person wanting to build stonewalls today is confronted with more re-strictions than existed over a century ago. At that time, there was no problem taking sea stones to add to different texture to the wall. Today, the State of New Hampshire frowns deeply upon such an activity. Beyond that, one must know how deep to dig to set the wall, how frost might effect drainage, and much more.

OLD IRONSIDES

The U.S.S. Constitution is berthed in Boston Harbor.
It is just as majestic today as it was when it was
commissioned in 1797.

Okay, it's late spring. It's top down weather (if you happen to have a rag top). You're cruising around Boston. What's the first thing that comes to your mind? Fenway Park? The clubs? Adopting a cat? Nah. Old Ironsides. Yeah, that's the ticket!

The U.S.S. Constitution is berthed in Boston Harbor. It is just as majestic today as it was when it was commissioned in 1797. It got the nickname, Old Ironsides, because the British cannonballs simply bounced off of her. Tough old lady, huh?

The ship was the first of the original six frigates to make up the United States Navy. And did she see action? You bet she did. She served in the undeclared war against France (1798-1800), and then in the Tripolitan War, and the War of 1812 . . . 42 battles in all!

By today's standards, she's bite-size. She's a little over 2,000 tons, once carried a crew of 450, and sports 44 major cannons. She was just a might formidable in the seagoing era in American history. The original intent of the vessel was to ward off pesky pirates from our nation's merchant vessels. You can almost smell the salt air and the acrid aroma of cannon smoke, can't you?

She was set to be scrapped in 1830, but Oliver Wendell Holmes wrote a tidy little piece about Old Ironsides. It won America's hearts and the old lady was saved. Here's the first stanza:

> Ay, tear her tattered ensign down
> Long has it waved on high,
> And many an eye has danced to see
> That banner in the sky;
> Beneath it rung the battle shout,
> And burst the cannon's roar; --
> The meteor of the ocean air
> Shall sweep the clouds no more.

Who could scrap her after stirring stuff like that? Whew!

Everyone has his or her own special moments once aboard the old ship (I truly believe no one comes away having had a bad experience.) My own personal highlight is simply feeling and hearing the ship creak on the gentle harbor waters. I let my imagination take over from there.

Below decks, I could almost hear the ghostly commands, "Beat to quarters!" and "Run out the guns!" I honestly get chills up my spine being that close to history.

There is no bad time to see the ship, but the real experience of Boston Harbor is not complete unless you take a free guided tour through the old battleship. If you're lucky, you just may find yourself aboard when Old Ironsides on the Fourth of July when the ship is slipped from its berth and turned in Boston Harbor. That little jaunt is necessary so that the ship may renew its commission for another year. And, if you're really lucky, the tall ships will be berthed along the piers beside her. Now, that's a treat!

LOBSTER TRAPS

Old wooden traps are more than just decorations –
they are tangible items of our culture.

A great part of the heritage of seacoast New England centers around the lobster industry. Native Americans used lobsters to fertilize fields and for fish bait. Early settlers brought them home by the basketful. The story goes that long ago, lobsters were as plentiful on New England beaches as seashells.

Time moved on. The demand crept higher and the numbers began to dwindle. Lobstermen had legal restrictions placed on their trade, but they continued to pursue the feast with great claws.

Currently, lobster traps are made of metal. They have a "one way" net door in one side, and a piece of fish hangs from the center of the lid. There really is not much personality to them. Not so with the traps of old.

Those babies were nearly two yards long and made of wooden slats fashioned into an arc around a flat slat base. When out of the water, these salt-seared relics have a certain magic about them that is just plain alluring.

Travelers along coastal highways never cease to grin at the nostalgia of old bait shots or small seafood shanties that have one or two tacked to the outside walls or stacked along the doorways. Clearly, New Englanders can't and won't let go of the past. Old wooden traps are more than just decorations – they are tangible items of our culture. Lobster trap Christmas trees still bring smiles to even the saltiest of old salts.

Don't be surprised if you find yourself eating off of one in some coastal resort. For some reason, it seems to make a steaming plate of scallops taste that much more delicious.

Not only are they found outside certain seaside businesses; they also make up part of the décor of some New England homes. If you're lucky enough to visit the abode of some old salt (or young salt, for that matter), you almost certainly will find his coffee table is fashioned from a trap that years ago may have been the demise of many bottom-dwelling denizens. By the way, they make great places to store and show a fisherman's library.

Walk through his kitchen. The bar along the side may feature three such traps covered with a glass top. The doors to his pantry . . . you guessed it. The only limit for old traps is an individual's imagination, and New Englanders have great imaginations. Just ask somebody here about the last fish he caught! And, one of the most creative uses for four traps . . . a wonderful writer's desk; it is definitely the perfect place for anyone to write "Son of

Moby."

The souvenir industry recognizes the love affair folks have with the traps. Go into almost any shop, and you will find miniature traps perfect to grace any desk or counter from Dallas to Denver. When asked about it, the owner will smile and gladly relate the story of his most recent New England adventure . . . and why not!

EDUCATION
NEW ENGLAND-STYLE

Harvard, Tufts, Bowdoin, Colby, Brown, Roger Williams, Yale, Wesleyan, Norwich, Middlebury, Dartmouth, and Saint Anselm are just a few.

The realm of New England (that's six not-so-huge states) is one-third the size of Texas. Within its borders are 164 major colleges and universities. That figure doesn't include junior colleges, community colleges, nursing schools, specialty schools or other centers of post-secondary education. They're schools in cities and towns in the region. Simply stated, that's a lot of schools with a lot of students to be crammed into a relatively small area.

You may have heard of a few of them. Harvard, Tufts, Bowdoin, Colby, Brown, Roger Williams, Yale, Wesleyan, Norwich, Middlebury, Clark, Dartmouth, and Saint Anselm are just a few. New England schools are top quality with top-notch instructors. It's no wonder that education in this region is a major business. Lots of money goes into schools, but major dollars are generated by them as well.

It is true that students not only come to these schools from all over the country, but from all over the world. They should. These places are institutions for thinkers. Let's face it. Some of our schools are over 350 years old. They've been dong something correctly for a very long time.

A great number of people from New England go on to schools of higher learning in the region. That's not surprising when one considers that according to the Morgan Quitano Press Education State Rankings 2005-2006, public schools in the area are the best in the country. Of the current top five, Vermont, Connecticut, Massachusetts, and Maine are ranked 1, 2, 3 and 5. (Somehow, New Jersey slipped in there at the fourth position.) New Hampshire and Rhode Island are ranked 15th and 16th respectively.

There are so many schools in the area that some campuses abut one another. Not surprisingly, in some metropolitan areas there are college consortiums. It is very conceivable that students can take a course from one school, two at another, and one or two a few blocks away. Talk about mixing and matching your education to suit your needs!

The students who go to colleges and universities in New England just don't have their noses in their books. Oh, no. Many of these fine young folks are student athletes. New England schools compete in sports in some well-known conferences: Atlantic Coast Conference, the Big East, the Atlantic 10 Conference, the Ivy League Conference, the Patriot League, the Northeast Conference, the Metro Atlantic Conference, the Colonial Athletic Association, and the American Conference. Take your pick; they're all great.

What seems to be true to me is that students and alumni of New England schools don't have to shout up their enthusiasm (except at sporting events, and then very loudly); they simply let their pride show in how they represent their schools and their region of the country . . . with a subtle confidence. Education is just another example of why New England pride is justified!

THE PERFECT GAME
FOR NEW ENGLAND

Seemingly, with every turn, he was chanting some sort
of numerical sequence, "Fifteen-two, fifteen-four . . .
and thirty-one for two."

It was late spring. It was the time of year when the shackles of winter were being forgotten for the promises of summer. The rumble of thunder was low, but ominous. I was finished delivering the Gazette and was wending my way through the streets of Main-South Worcester. An old man sat on his piazza smoking his pipe and beckoning as I passed by.

"Game? Game," he asked.

I glanced up at him. Growing up an urban kid, I had learned to take in a lot at a blink. He was heavyset and leaned heavily on a cane. At his elbow, he had a glass of iced tea resting on an end table. In front of him stood a block of wood, a deck of cards and an old tobacco can.

I mumbled something about not knowing how and kept walking. He coughed and called back, "When you finish, come back. I'll show you."

I nodded.

It was raining with a fury by the time I finished delivering my papers. As I raced up the street, I saw that the old man and another elderly gentleman were seated on the porch. The man who had invited me was having a jolly time. He chuckled with every turn of a card. Seemingly, with every turn, he was chanting some sort of numerical sequence, "Fifteen-two, fifteen-four . . . and thirty-one for two."

The other elderly gentleman was not having nearly as much fun as the first. Far from it. He was grumbling every few seconds and muttering words which, I was certain, were not part of the game. Every so often, the first old man would use a stubby pencil to jot some figures on a small pad. He would then chuckle some more. The more he chuckled, the more the other grumbled. And, the rain came down in torrents. And, the lightning flashed. And, the thunder roared. I was learning cribbage.

The game had its origin in 17th century England and was invented by a poet. The pilgrims brought the game to these shores. It has been a New England passion ever since.

It is a simple game, really. I won't go into all of the details, but it involves the movement of pegs into holes on a small wooden board. The progression of numbers, suits, pairs, trips, or runs determine how many times the pegs will be moved. The numbers 15 and 31 are considered to be sacred. There are skunks in the game. They don't smell, but they do make a player feel very badly.

Those two old men were playing for a penny a point. Money is not an essential element of the game. The thrill really is having your pegs outrace your opponent's to the finish line. No horse race has more spectacular finishes than many a game of cribbage.

Long into a winter's night or during a rainy afternoon at the beach, couples, kids, or old crones will pass the time of day while chanting their way to the 121st hole.

Peg boards come in all manner of shapes and sizes. Most are wooden and simply constructed. Old timers seem to prefer this board. Newbies like to move plastic pegs around a board possibly shaped like the state of New Hampshire. I know a gentleman who has quite a collection of boards, some dating back to the American Revolution, but he doesn't play the game! Frankly, I think he's missing an exquisite joy.

Now, back to my tale . . . sometime later I did see the two men playing again on the same front porch. It was another rainy afternoon, almost a carbon copy of the first. Nearly identical, but for one small item . . . the other man was doing the cackling!

CRANBERRIES - MORE THAN A THANKSGIVING SIDE DISH

Today, mechanized "egg beaters" are brought in.

Cape Cod is the most perfect growing environment in the world. Cape Cod was given to New England with compliments from the last Ice Age. As a little added bonus, Mother Nature threw in just the perfect environment to grow a most wonderful treat – cranberries. You see, to grow those precious little gems, several items are essential: natural peat and a frosty water temperature. According to the experts, Cape Cod is the most perfect growing environment in the world.

New Englanders had been harvesting wild cranberries for years, but it wasn't until 1816 when Henry Hall began to cultivate the crop by moving wild plants to sandy soil that an industry was developed. By the 1840's, serious techniques in harvesting the "pearl of the bog" came into being. And, by the 1860's, the first commercial bog was developed. At Harwich, a bog was discovered with berries so richly red, they appeared black.

Fall is the traditional harvest time, even for cranberries. In the past, long lines of people would stand knee deep in bogs and use long "combs" attached to small baskets to scoop up the crop. Today, mechanized "egg beaters" are brought in. A person stands atop this odd-looking water buggy and directs multiple water reels to shake the vines to loosen the berries. The vines then float to the top of the water and are later basketed and taken away in trucks.

Today, the cranberry is the largest agricultural crop in Massachusetts. Of the thousand growers in the country, more than half of them are located in the Bay State. That's actually a very small number when you come to think of it.

Anyone who has devoured a traditional New England Thanksgiving feast will attest to the fact that cranberries (the red cylindrical glob that slides out of a can) are delicious and perfect company for a turkey leg. But, is it beneficial to your health? You bet it is. Tradition has it that New England sailors used to carry it aboard ship to help prevent scurvy. Scientists today recognize the true benefits of the cranberry in fighting many forms of cancer, as well as being vitamin rich. In fact, the cranberry just might be considered the healthiest food in the world. Oddly enough, it is only grown in a mere handful of places worldwide.

Besides being found in a morning glass of juice and annual repasts, the cranberry is finding its way into a number of meals which grace New England tables: atop chicken; flavoring a glazed ham; adding zest to spiced pork, and even sprinkled atop a sausage pizza are just a few.

As a treat, "They're good and good fer ya." Pies, cakes, cookies and truffles are now fair game. And, if you don't want to go to the trouble of whipping them into some fine concoction, you can always devour a bag or two of the dried variety while watching the movie of your choice.

If you're in the neighborhood, you might drop into almost any breakfast shop down on the Cape and order up a batch of cranberry pancakes with hot cranberry syrup and a side order of sausage patties. It's almost guaranteed, you'll close your eyes as you savor each mouthful.

Oh, and yes, Virginia, the cranberry is a vegetable.

NEW ENGLAND FISHING YA' GOTTA LOVE IT!

For me, nothing beats the taste of
nearly any fish from the northeast.

My cousins took Child Bride and me to dinner last night. I could see a near beatific smile creep across my beloved's face as she savored her halibut. She leaned against my shoulder and whispered some headline news.

"I'm becoming a real fish person!"

This is not a bad line from a vintage horror flick. No, far from it. You see, Child Bride is from the Four Corners region of the American Southwest. Being a true westerner (She boasts of having sat upon John Wayne's knee.), she loves her steaks . . . thick . . . medium well, and often. Now, for her boldly to state (okay, so she whispered it?) that she was loving the taste of fish from our "garden," is a great step in her conversion toward becoming a true New Englander (I still can't get her to say, "chowdah").

For me, nothing beats the taste of nearly any fish from the northeast. With the Atlantic at our front door, and six states filled with lakes, rivers, ponds, streams and brooks of frosty waters, the chances are excellent that good things will grow there.

I don't really believe that Child Bride actually had to work to acquire a taste for fish. I knew that once we became settled here, it was just going to happen. Oh, and here's another bulletin, just in . . . "New England has great sea food restaurants, too!"

Growing up I one of the region's heavily urban areas, I was frequently able to see some truly amazing sights. One of which was the Friday night 'fish 'n chips' lines at a local eatery. What made it so fascinating was that it was nothing to find a businessman standing behind a construction worker, standing behind a fashion model, standing behind a motorcycle tough . . . out the door, around the corner and down the block. The haddock became the great equalizer. It was delicious.

Another common sight nearly anywhere in the most wonderful corner of America is families going off to the ocean, to the woods, or up a trail into the mountains. And, what are those items sticking out of their backpacks? You know it . . . fishing rods. Moms and pops have been teaching their kids how to tie a hook, or change a spoon, or shift out a lure since fish were invented. Nearly every kid, urban or rural alike, can fillet a trout and have it pan-fried in garlic and butter before you can say "Martha Stewart."

The Atlantic is a bountiful provider. Lobster, haddock, scrod, blue, scallops and clams are just a few of the denizens you're sure to meet, eat and enjoy. Inland, you'll catch and digest trout (nearly all kinds), bass, horned pout (catfish to you non-locals) pike and more. Oh, there are limitations on size, amount and seasons to fish. Yes, you may have to shell out a few dollars for a license. And, yes, you have to be careful not to go traipsing across somebody's lawn while you're trying to nab a perch, but that's about it in the way of restrictions.

For the record, there are no restrictions on licenses needed for telling fish stories. New England abounds in 'em. Frankly, I never put too much stock in 'em. Most are just tall tales. All mine, however, are completely true. Did I ever tell you the story of my six-foot northern pike that I pulled out of the Quabbin Reservoir? No?

Well, it was the fall of the year. A little wind was beginning to whip in front the west. I was making my last cast, and I thought I snagged a stump. Well, I . . .

ANOTHER FISH STORY

I truly love fishing. I love fishing New England.
I love it even with I get skunked.

I read someplace that the definition of a fisherman is "a jerk at one end of the line waiting for a jerk at the other." Okay, so call me a jerk. I truly love fishing. I love fishing New England. I love it even with I get skunked. (It is a lot better, however, to catch something.)

Weather doesn't bother me. Just let me find a body of water with the possibility of something lurking underneath, and I'm a happy camper . . . more aptly, a happy fisherman.

I haven't fished all of New England. That prospect alone gives me a reason to live a long, long time. There are lots of bodies of water in this blessed region, and so many of them have lunkers hunkering (alliteration intended) near the bottom just waiting for me to toss in a line.

I would be less than truthful, and would cause raging debates, if I were to state boldly that I knew the best place to fish in the six-state region. Here's how, the argument would begin: "Best? Best how . . . most fish . . . biggest fish . . . most scenic . . . cleanest air . . . Places where you've had the best times?" Uh-uh, not me. I'm not going down that bear trail. Suffice to say, from northernmost Maine to southernmost Connecticut, there is some kind of fishing to please just about everyone. (Sorry, there's always someone out there who is not pleased by anything.)

Let's start with the big pond to the east . . . the Atlantic Ocean. How do you want to fish it? From shore? From a jetty? From a dingy? A trawler? For my money, no fish tastes better than a fish pulled out of the North Atlantic. From the Gulf of Maine, to Buzzard's Bay, to Narragansett Bay, it's a great place to fish. Cod, haddock, blue, salmon, flounder and the list goes on and on. What a treat!

Child Bride and I took an excursion on a charter boat for some mackerel fishing. What an amazing day! Believe it or not, not one of us on board used bait. Almost as fast as we could drop a line into the water, we pulled out a fish. In the matter of a few hours, all of the ice chests were filled.

And, in no particular order, there's stream fishing, lake fishing and ice fishing. I will admit, I haven't tried sitting by a hole in a bobhouse on the ice waiting for a hungry fish (see definition), but I'm game. I'll try anything once. Twice, if I get lucky.

Like most fishermen, I have some great stories to tell about the big one that got away. Mine are different. Mine are true. I don't want to regale you with all of them, let me just share this one. An elderly gentleman neighbor and I went fishing in the Wachusett Reservoir in central Massachusetts. We were going after horned pout (catfish, to you non-New Englanders). Yours truly was not having any luck, while my neighbor was wearing out his wrist reeling them in. He was filling a bucket, while I practiced my cursing. Suddenly, I had a bite. Nothing spectacular, just a slight tug. I began to reel in, but there was no resistance. The old man and I laughed at my bad luck, until the fish broke water. It was huge! A land-locked northern pike, and over three feet long. It flew out of the water like a surface-to-air missile, and promptly knocked over the old man's bucket of fish. The monster and the escapees all made it safely back into the water, while Mr. Chuckles and I tried to pick ourselves out of the dirt. No last laugh. No fish. But what a great time!

Bodies of water are nearly as plentiful as maple leaves in New England. Next to a great book and a bowl of tobacco, I can't think of a more relaxing way to spend a few hours than by fishing . . . I wonder if that lurking lunker in Wachusett is still yukking it up with his cronies . . . telling them his version of that fishing story.

THE ARTS AND ARTISANS
OF NEW ENGLAND

It is a common enough sight throughout New England to come upon someone sitting by the side of the road, or on a stump or on a stonewall to be busily engrossed in sketching, painting or penning.

I have travelled extensively about the country. From what I gather, many Americans outside of New England believe that the people of this region are stiff and abrupt. In short . . . not nice folks. I guess the thought was that since I'm generally a nice guy, I most certainly must have been escaping the area. Did they think I lived near Yankee Stadium? Nothing that I could say could convince anyone that all of those angry myths about the horrors of the region are just that . . . myths.

From my perspective, it must be next to impossible to live in the wondrous region of New England and not have that perspective show in our lives, in our relations with others, and in our art. In my view, the art of the region is the region. It is a living canvas. It is a spectrum of colors, a cosmos of shapes, temperatures and textures. In a conversation I had with Child Bride prior to moving here, I sad, "If a person cannot be creative in some form or other here, his or her heart must have stopped beating a very long time ago."

It is a common enough sight throughout New England to come upon someone sitting by the side of the road or on a stump or on a stonewall to be busily engrossed in sketching, painting or penning something sparked by the vista at hand. New Englanders, and those who visit the region, try to capture the sights, the smells . . . essentially, the feelings of the area in some form of their human artistic productions.

Route 1A meanders along the coastline. As it passes through Rye, New Hampshire, it bends around a small marina nestled in among large granite boulders. Faded wooden buoys bob in the water to mark the entrance to the spot. Gulls spiral overhead. The smell of the sea is fragrant. In short, it is a very charming bit of New England. From late spring through late fall, artists and would-be artists search out just the correct angle to capture their visions. I have seen the same sailboats captured by thousands of people in thousands of ways. All of the artists smile as they produce their labors of love. New England truly does bring out the best in people, both from their personalities and from their souls.

Child Bride likes to drag me along to arts and crafts shows any and everywhere she finds one. From Ogunquit to P'town and from Sunapee to Spencer, we hit them all! I dutifully grump a little, but the truth is I really enjoy going. I am always amazed at what regional folks can do with just about anything they find lying about. They turn ancient fence posts into birdhouses, yardsticks into stools and snow skis into chairs. I'm always a little saddened after I go to one of these events thinking, "I just tossed away a bunch of those. I could've made a windmill." My second thought is, "Get real, buddy, you hardly know which end of the hammer to hold."

After I recover from my momentary remorse, admiration for the artists and their labors takes over. I spend hours examining the photographs, paintings, carvings, sculptures and what-nots at these festivals. Child Bride spends as much time trying to drag me out as she did trying to drag me in. More actually, I'm sure it's longer. I can't get enough of those events. I really can't. I may not have the best taste in art (Child Bride say, "Yeah, you got that right"), but I do know what I like, and I do marvel at the abilities of so many everyday folk in the region who produce great stuff (remember, in my estimation only). New England has its famous artists, centuries of them. I do appreciate, however, the manner in which most folks in the area are making art a part of their lives. If they're not doing it, they're certainly looking at it. And, yes, that is very, very good.

Here's my advice: Find a local artist sketching a tree in mid-October. Do you feel your pulse begin to slow? Watch the artist lather the work with the vibrant colors of fall. Do you feel your shoulders unknot? Watch the artist shade the bark on the trunk. Do you feel your breathing begin to deepen?

If you think watching is great, grab up a brush and daub it on some canvas. You're feeling a lot better already. Aren't you.

THE SUNKEN FOREST OF RYE

The trees were all over 100 years old. Further, the
stumps have been carbon dated, which indicates
the trees were alive some 3,600 years ago.

There's a great cedar forest in Rye, New Hampshire . . . or at least there used to be one. At extremely low tides, the stumps of this once-great forest can be found, just northeast of Jenness Beach. It has to be an extremely low ebb tide, however, because the last times they were exposed in recent history were in 1940, 1958, 1962, 1978 . . . and 2004. Child Bride and I have actually seen them!

This might have been a truly mighty forest, for the stumps of these trees measure between 8-10 feet in circumference. When the stumps were last visible, the rings on the 56 found were counted. The trees were all over 100 years old. Further, the stumps have been carbon dated, which indicates the trees were alive some 3,600 years ago (give or take 200 years). In all probability, the stumps were submerged when the early settlers arrived; no mention of them is recorded from the Colonial era.

There is speculation as to how large the forest may have been. Current thinking is that the Atlantic rose after the last ice age, and the New England of that era appeared quite different from what we know today. It is highly possible that what is now the New Hampshire coastline was actually some miles inland from the ocean at that time. Best estimates are that the shoreline might have been up to 75 miles east of where it is at present. If true, it may have been possible for early hunters to walk from southern Cape Cod to Nantucket Island without putting their feet in the Atlantic Ocean. One clue that points in that direction is that the stumps of the cedars and pines currently underwater do not thrive if their roots are in salt water.

A similar "sunken forest," or part of the same, is located just south of Oriorne's Point. It is not as sunken as the one at Rye and is visible at many low tides. At present, there is no indication how far these forests may extend to the east. One indication that a vast forest existed is that fishermen in the region have hauled up the teeth of mastodons and mammoths dozens of miles from shore.

Interestingly enough, the last few yards of the Transatlantic Cable may have been laid directly through the sunken forest. The Amabassadore brought the cable from the Faraday and up to the beach on July 15,

1874. There is no indication thatit had suffered any damages, since messages were sent to Europe using the cable almost immediately.

There is a small green sign on the side of the road in Rye. It marks the location of both the sunken forest and the Old Cable House. Both the sunken forest and the Cable House are representative of the wonders of the history of New England and southern New Hampshire in particular.

STONE QUARRIES
OF NEW ENGLAND

Spend some time in New England, and you will spy a stone wall. Those walls are made of granite, and the granite came from right below your feet.

Many homegrown New England guys know where some abandoned quarries are. Most us spent some parts of our early summers diving into these terrific granite swimming pools. They were wonderful. The water was always refreshing and clean, and the rocks around them offered the perfect place to bike. I haven't been part of the swimming hole scene for over four decades now; I just hope the current batch of kids have as much fun as I did so many moons ago.

Spend some time in New England, and you will spy a stone wall. Those walls are made of granite, and the granite came from right below your feet. Where there are small stones, you might expect to find larger ones . . . and still larger ones . . . and some larger than that! Even though New Hampshire is called the Granite State, it does not corner the market on all of the granite in the region. And, where there are large formations of granite, you're quite likely to find a quarry.

New Englanders have been prying rocks from the ground since before New England was called New England. In 1749, the quarry business was certainly crude by today's standards. Back then, folks would drop large iron balls on heated stones, just hoping that they would crack. If that occurred, the pieces could be forced away and tooled down. As time passed, the industry grew and became more technologically advanced.

The quarry industry was in the perfect place at the perfect time to benefit the growth of New England and the country. With readily-available water transport, slabs of granite could be shipped to help create virtually any structure designed to last. Everything from railroad bridges to post offices, and from statues to cobblestones for roads, came from the great walls of granite in the region. Seemingly, there was a never-ending supply of the stuff, as well as a never-ending need for it.

The industry grew through the Civil War era and beyond. The country was expanding, and the need for granite seemed assured. But, like all good things, the end was in sight. In the late 1820's, the use of brick began to take over. It was nearly as sturdy a material and easily made and shipped.

There have been some peaks and valleys in the granite industry and a lot of constants. Stone for decorative purposes (including the current trend in counter tops), tombstones and some construction still is vital to the granite industry, but for the most part, the great need for granite as the giant industry of the northeast is long over.

Many of the quarries of yesteryear are simply the swimming holes of today with one slight addendum. Rock climbing has become a passion for outdoor enthusiasts, and what better place to go climb a rock than in some abandoned quarry. There are rock climbing clubs throughout the region; and, on any given weekend, you can find their members scurrying up and down the walls of the places where some of the most beautiful stone in the country was freed.

If you can't find a rock-climbing club to find the closest quarry, ask most any kid in any town in the great northeast. He'll tell you. Bring a towel or a pick axe . . . your choice.

New England rocks!

THINGS MAPLE

Maple products from New England
maple trees just taste good.

Yes, I'm well aware that maple trees outside of New England produce enough sap to make an adequate and somewhat tasty batch of maple syrup. And, yes, I understand that some of those trees grow in the land of the pinstripes. But let's face it. "Hmmm, boy! Real New York Maple Syrup! I can't wait!" Nah, I don't think so.

Don't ask me what it is . . . the sweetness of the air . . . the richness of the soil . . . the love affair between the tree growers and their trees . . . maybe all of the above, but maple products from New England maple trees just taste good.

You've seen them, haven't you? The folks are heading back to Kalamazoo or Kansas City, and they've got a maple-shaped bottle sitting in the back window of their car or in the middle of their carry-on luggage.

"Ah, I see you've been to Vermont."

"Oh, yes, the missus and I had a great time. We were going to bring back some of that maple sugar candy and maple butter . . . "

"Bet it didn't make it back to the motel, did it?"

"You got that right. We were bringing it back for the kids and the neighbors. But, heck, they didn't pay for the vacation. We did!"

"My sentiments exactly!"

Vermont produces a quarter of all of the maple syrup sold in the United States. Now, keep in mind that it takes about 40 gallons of raw sap to produce one gallon of eatable syrup. A mature maple tree produces about 10 gallons of sap each season. The season is between four to six weeks long at the end of February and into March. Does that give you a clue about the numbers of maple trees in the region?

If you will allow me a slight digression here . . . all those calendars you see for McMurdy's Funeral Home or Joe's Gas Station featuring a gorgeous fall vista of maples in the height of their magnificent colored plumage is not trick photography. Those are the trees in the region. It's beautiful here!

Now, where was I? Ah, yes. Maple trees . . . there is a bit of a debate over which produces the better syrup – the black maple or the sugar maple. Frankly, I don't know a single New Englander who has checked into that argument. We really don't care which trees it comes from, we just like our maple syrup.

A terrific photo op (and, the trees will pose for you) is during the harvest time. Vast numbers of trees appear with buckets attached to nails. Those nails (or spikes or hollow tubes) are the channels for the rich amber-colored fluid to reach the buckets.

I won't go through the whole process, but suffice to say that the sugar shack which turns sap into a most tasty concoction smells delicious. A tip for the traveller here: take a scoop of snow and pour some freshly-made hot syrup on top of it. Oh my! You can thank me later. You'll find those shacks and accompanying goodies shops all over most northern highways.

Do yourself a favor, pull over and step inside. Oh, and if you're really feeling generous, try to remember to bring some maple sugar candy, or butter, or syrup home to someone who didn't make the trip . . . even if they didn't help to pay for the gas.

DO WE HAVE SPORTS? YOU BET!

Like sports? You'll love New England. The games
are here. The fans are here. The championships are here.
What are you waiting for?

Forgive me if I seem to be gloating, proud member of Red Sox Nation that I am. (Hey, Pinstripers, remember them? They're the only team in professional baseball to have won three World Championships in the new millennium!) Okay, don't forgive me; I'm still proud. Let's face it, New Englanders have a few athletic accomplishments on which to hang our hats.

Ever head of a little team called the 'Celtics'? No? You need to have cable under that rock. The Celts have won 16 championships, 8 of which were in a row. That just happens to be the longest streak of consecutive championships in U.S. sports history. If I weren't at the "Gahden" catching a game, I had Johnny Most plugged into my ear from my handy transistor radio. Talk about a team! Bill Russell, Bob Cousy, K.C. Jones, and on, and on, and on. I think I acquired my taste for a fine cigar every now and then from the look of sheer pleasure on Coach Red Auerbach's face each time he lit up a victory stogie. Believe me, he fired up quite a few!

Not into basketball? How about football? How about those New England Patriots? Not quite a dynasty yet, but they do play the game! Hard, fast, and with a flair! They had their lean years, and they may well have been called the Nomads of New England, but the Pats certainly have found a home in Foxboro, Massachusetts. Beginning in 1960, the Pats have been nothing if not colorful. The crowds always came, even if the victories didn't. Then, a new millennium, a new attitude. Bill Belichick took the helm and the real glory years began. Four Super Bowl wins in fourteen years is not just a small accomplishment. These are the "Brady Bunch' years. Tom is the field general and the commander-in-chief of the offense. If you don't like precision and a thinking man's game plan, you will absolutely hate the Patriots. They find the way to win.

What about that other Garden team, the Boston Bruins? This is the National Hockey League's blue collar lunch pail team. They play hockey the way it was intended to be played . . . with an attitude. And that attitude is all about winning. Taking to the ice in 1924, they've been in the playoffs 62 times, won 21 division championships, four conference championships, and five league championships. (That's the Stanley Cup, probably the most kissed bit of hardware in sports.) My glory years as a fan were '69 through '72. They had it all . . . Bobby Orr, Phil Esposito, Wayne Cashman, Pie McKenzie and a cast of characters who enjoyed the game, playing it with reckless abandon. I was a gallery god back then. Simply put, you hung out over the ice (about five stories up) and screamed your lungs out with every shot, every check and every goal. I have to admit, I'm sort of a fallen away Bruins' fan in recent years. Living 30+ years in the Sun Belt will do that to you, but I'm back. And, so are the Bruins.

New England sports fans never have to want for action. There's always a great professional game going on somewhere in the splendid tract of land called New England. Tickets for the bigs may be scarce. Major and minor cities in the region, however, do provide a ton of great minor-league action for your entertainment dollar. The Worcester Ice Cats, the Pawtucket Red Sox (longest game in professional baseball history), and the Mohegan Wolves (arena football) are just a few.

If you like sports, you'll love New England. The games are here. The fans are here. The championships are here. What are you waiting for?

MILLS AND FACTORIES
OF NEW ENGLAND

*No one could have designed a better locale than this region for
the brown brick buildings of the early 1800's.*

The Industrial Age is long over and many of the mills and factories of that
era are now condominiums, boutiques or artist's studios. The skies are clean
today. The chimneys that once belched smoke stand quietly against a blue
New England sky.

No one could have designed a better locale than this region for the brown
brick buildings of the early 1800's. The Atlantic was at the doorstep. What
goods were needed could be easily shipped in, while the finished products
from cities and towns could be shipped out. Lumber from the many forests of
the area was readily available for fuel or construction purposes. Granite was
certainly in abundance to build the massive factories. Nearly every shovel
driven into soil found a rock of some size. The region is laced with numerous
rivers and streams and dotted with lakes and ponds; a power source and another source of transport were right there in our own backyards. Finally, the
region was one of the primary locations for immigrants to the United States
to live and find readily-available work. At least 39 cities and towns on some of
the seven major rivers were considered to be mill or factory towns.

The factories were not always the most wonderful places to work. Injuries
and accidents were commonplace. The laws that protect the workers of today
weren't even on the books in those days. Folks worked long and strenuous
hours at factories that might be only a few short steps from their tenement
houses. The houses were, for the most part, three-deckers. Many of them
were owned by the factories.

Textiles, furniture, metal products . . . virtually anything that could be
produced in factories were produced in New England. Household goods,
tools, products large and small left the region by truck, wagon, ship, train
and plane. The region thrived because of the muscle that produced the items
necessary to build the nation.

Goods are still produced here, but essentially the mill mentality is gone.
The economy of the region comes from diverse sources now. The change has
been a good one for new England. Fish are returning to the waterways. The
air is sweet-smelling. And, not everything depends on the last pair of shoes
shipped from a dingy factory in a rough corner of a northeast city.

Those shoes, however, may be worn on the feet of someone dancing to the latest beat on a dance floor which might have housed some loud, oil-spewing machinery in the past century. The factory next door might now house a wonderful ethnic restaurant, and the one on the corner might be the home of a terrific bookstore, apartments or artists' studios. The traces of the past, however, are definitely there. The factories and the signs still indicate the building had a real history. The new life for the factories and mills of yester-year is probably the most remarkable makeover on record.

Visit one, or two, or ten. You'll definitely enjoy your time there. Oh, and if you really like them, you may consider moving into one. Many have been turned into condominiums, and they're beautiful.

COBBLESTONE STREETS
BELONG IN NEW ENGLAND

Courtesy is the byword on these streets.

Many folks believe that cobblestone streets are unique to New England. Sorry, we in the glorious Northeast can't take credit for that. Still other folks believe that cobblestone streets must have come from England in Colonial times. That's partially true. The original cobblestone streets of New England were set in place before Paul Revere made sparks on his famous midnight ride, but England can't claim to be the birthplace of these roads. No, the first cobblestone streets probably came into existence in ancient Mesopotamia, some six or seven thousand years ago. (I'm not going to argue with anyone who finds a cobblestone street someplace else, which might be a week or two older.)

The reality is that they do look darn good right here in old New England. Many towns and cities of the area still have them and maintain them very well. I will tell you, they do not make driving always a pleasurable experience. Your shocks may get quite a workout dribbling down one of these quaint little roads. Your body, however, will thank you for taking it over a cobblestone street. The stones actually massage your feet, and a walk along them can positively alter your blood pressure. Frankly, I'm not convinced if walking the streets will actually improve your health, but the sights, sounds and smells along the street enhance your general sense of well-being. Sounds like a great debate for a Harvard medical forum, doesn't it?

Not every thoroughfare in this terrific six-state region is made of cobblestones. Far from it. New England can boast of some of the most modern roads in the country. They are a breeze to drive on, and are easily accessible, too. Truth is, you can get there from here!

No, cobblestone streets are found in some parts of many towns and cities with current ties to their historical roots. From Bar Harbor, Maine to Newport, Rhode Island, and so many areas in between, communities can brag that they have decided to keep their cobblestones without paving them over. So many of these streets were originally designed for carriages, so don't expect to find them to be ultra-wide. Courtesy is the byword on these streets. A driver may have to let one or several cars dominate the road going in the opposite direction before he or she can maneuver along.

Further, those who suffer from claustrophobia might be advised that the buildings (usually red brick) are located just about an arm's length from the street. Folks paid taxes based on frontage way back when. Frankly, I believe the more accessible they are, the better. More often than not, these same streets house some of the most wonderful shops, restaurants and taverns than their more spacious, twenty-first century cousins in other parts of the country. They are truly the memory lanes of simpler times.

Don't be surprised to find families really enjoying their lives in these streets. In the North End of Boston, some of the greatest stickball games in the world are played atop the same streets the Redcoats trod over some two-hundred years ago. My guess is that those kids enjoy those games much more than those soldiers enjoyed marching.

So, the next time someone tells you to take a hike, take him up on it . . . but do it on a cobblestone street.

KEEPING AN EYE ON THE SKY

On a cold day in March of 1926, Robert
Goddard launched Nell skyward.

New Englanders accept the fact that so much of their lives revolve around the sky. Storms, growing cycles, even how we dress to watch the Pats in Foxboro depends on how keenly we are aware of what's happening in the heavens above. Some have gone literally miles beyond just being aware; they have raised the bar several notches in terms of what may be going on slightly above terra firma.

On a cold day in March of 1926, Robert Goddard launched Nell skyward. 2.5 seconds later; the small rocket crashed into a cabbage field in Auburn, Massachusetts. Thus, the era of liquid-fuel rocketry was underway. In less than a century, the world accepted that space travel was not just a probability, but a certainty. Many of the questions that exist for the future of the planet may be found in the heavens, and we are searching for the answers.

The Worcester area's involvement in space ventures didn't cease with Nell. Far from it. Several industries in the area continue to be a vital part of the space venture. Wyman-Gordon Company manufactures parts for Saturn rockets. Along with the David Clark Company, they produce many of the fittings for the aluminum engines and lunar modules. The Supernant Cable Corporation of Clinton produces cables for the launch support systems. The Sprague Electric Company produces much of the micro-technology for the space industry which included the disc that left on the moon. The Norton Company supplies many of the small pieces which are so essential to the giant rockets. Honematic Machine of Boylston produces aluminum alloys for the cylinders and struts for the lunar module.

New England just doesn't lend itself to the hardware of the frontier of space. There is very much a human aspect as well.

We will never forget the lunar nine iron shots made by Alan Shepard. The native of Derry, New Hampshire had commanded the Apollo 14 flight, and was the only astronaut of the Mercury Seven team to walk on the moon.

Christa McAuliffe was born on September 2, 1948 in Framingham, Massachusetts. She was a jogger, a swimmer, a Girl Scout leader and a teacher. While teaching at Concord High School in Concord, New Hampshire, she applied and was accepted into the Teacher in Space program. Out of 11,500 applicants, she was chosen! After many hours of rigorous training, she joined the crew of seven to fly aboard the Challenger Space Shuttle. On January 28,

1986, the mission ended tragically. Her message to the world, however, was simple and poignant, "I touch the future, I teach." Christa was certainly a gallant space pioneer.

30,000 children a year visit the Christa McAuliffe Planetarium in Concord, New Hampshire. The facility offers all the opportunity to view and understand better the majesty of space.

In Main South Worcester, Massachusetts, the birthplace of Robert Goddard, is a memorial to the man. Its centerpiece is a stainless steel abstract of a rocket on a launching pad. It is not an overwhelming tribute, but it does serve to mark his landmark achievement in world history.

Both of these sites remind us that dreams can be realized and goals, no matter how enormous, can be achieved. New Englanders are committed to making a better tomorrow by the efforts they put forth today.

HURRICANES AND TORNADOES

*It may be safe to say that the terrain
limits the life span of such storms.*

Certainly, the wonderful northeastern region of the United States is not considered to be Tornado Alley. The Prairie States have that dubious distinction. This is not to say that over the years a few haven't touched down here.

Since 1950, Maine has recorded 88 storms. From those, only one fatality has been recorded. Only two of those storms may have achieved an E-2 status (winds between 113-157 mph).

In that same time period, Vermont had only 34 storms, but two of those may have achieved F-4 status (207-260 mph) or greater. Of the eight tornadoes endured by Rhode Island, only one may have achieved any significant size. Conversely, Connecticut had 67 storms, including a significant number of F-3 and F-4 haymakers. Only one life was lost in all of those storms. Massachusetts appears to be the record holder with nearly 150 storms in that time period. Although there have been no F-5 monsters, there have been several to achieve F-4 status.

What the effects of global warming are has yet to be decided, but it may no longer be fair to say that tornadoes are foreign to the region. If there is a positive here, it may be safe to say that the terrain limits the life span of such storms.

On the Fourth of July, 1898, folks in Hampton Beach, New Hampshire were enjoying the holiday. The biggest events of the day were the presentations from the stereopticon projector in the former skating rink. About 3:00 p.m., a very large and powerful tornado slammed into the building. A total of nine persons were killed in the possible F-5 storm.

Folks in Worcester, Massachusetts still talk about THE TORNADO of July 9, 1953 as though it happened yesterday. This monster hugged the valleys and created a corridor of death and destruction throughout the county.

New England isn't immune from swirling storms coming in from the seas. The numbers of hurricanes to hit the region from 1900 to present pale in comparison to its tornadic cousins. There have been some 24 storms, but only a handful has packed a punch strong enough to cause significant damage. The "Hurricane of '38", by any standards, was a tremendously bad storm. The destruction and loss of life was certainly beyond belief. In tree damage alone, some 2.7 broad feet were felled.

This translates into millions upon millions of trees! Hollywood's "The Perfect Storm" depicts the violent collision between a snowstorm and a hurricane in 1991. New Englanders aren't likely to forget that blow anytime soon.

As with tornadoes, global warming may impact the numbers and sizes of hurricanes which may drop in uninvited to the shores of New England.

I gave careful consideration to: (a.) writing this piece, and (b.) including it with so many of New England's tales of glory. My rationale for its inclusion is that these storms are part and parcel of the reality of New England life. If one were to buy a particular piece of property, s/he would be delighted to have an honest disclosure sheet for the property. So, Gentle Reader, please do consider this short piece your buyer disclosure sheet for treacherous storms in the area.

Yeah, we got 'em, but I wouldn't worry about 'em. More often than not, weather stories make great fodder for the six o'clock news, and not much more needs to be said about them. Now, if a twister were to approach Fenway Park, and the Sox were behind the Yanks 4-3 in the top of the fifth . . . then, my friend, you've got a weather story!

THE SWAN BOATS OF THE BOSTON PUBLIC GARDENS

But, if you like your enjoyment of the quiet and mellow variety, you just may wish to set sail with the swans.

I'm a nut for opening days. I used to look forward to the opening day of fishing season with a passion; I was sure if I weren't on some shore in the wee hours of the first day, I was going to lose "my" catch to someone else.

Opening day for the Red Sox at the Fen is equally as special. After the traditional festivities, the magical words, "PLAY BALL!" would initiate the start of another season of baseball. It was as though I hadn't aged a day since last season. Another pennant? Maybe.

There is another opening day which goes virtually unheralded in Boston; its beginnings in the late 1800's. The season actually begins on April 15th and closes on September 17th. You might be thinking it has to be regular-season baseball, but you'd be wrong. It's actually the swan boat season in Boston Public Gardens.

For the nominal price of $2.75 for adults, $1.25 for kids, and $2.00 if you're my age, you can enjoy 15 minutes of bliss on the peaceful lagoon waters in the heart of the Hub City.

In the 1870's, Robert Paget had a simple idea to delight those who enjoyed the spring greenery of Boston. Essentially, all he did was to harness the power of a bicycle to two pontoons connected by slats of wood. He fashioned a large swan to cover the "power" and the person peddling. As many as six benches facing forward were placed in front of the swan, and the swan boat was born. The small boats, carrying as many as 20 passengers at a time, became an immediate hit, and folks flocked (pun intended) to cruise the park. The course is about two miles long and goes under a small walking bridge at one point.

Paget had his idea from the boats from an opera by Lohengrin. Sadly, Paget lived only a year after the inception of his idea, but his family has continued to carry on the swan boat tradition. Interestingly, the swan boats were featured in the stories Make Way for Ducklings and The Trumpet of the Swan. Even more interestingly, they are the only boats of their kind in the world.

Swans (the real ones) were released into Boston Public Garden in 1909. Between 1910 and 1912, swans were introduced to the lower Hudson Valley and Long Island. It may be assumed that the popularity of the swan boats in Boston had a direct bearing on these incidents.

Chances are, there will be wildly enthusiastic crowds at Fenway on opening day, and every day thereafter throughout the baseball season. But, if you like your enjoyment of the quiet and mellow variety, you just may wish to set sail with the swans. For, even though the Sox may disappoint their fans every now and again, the Swans never do.

GROTON IS BIG SEA COUNTRY

The Turtle failed in its mission to sink H.M.S. Eagle
with an armed mine, but the message was clear.
Submarine warfare was here to stay.

The Turtle was designed by Yale student, David Bushnell. It was a one-man attack submarine used against the British in the Revolutionary War. The Turtle failed in its mission to sink H.M.S. Eagle with an armed mine, but the message was clear. Submarine warfare was here to stay.

Let's fast-forward a couple of hundred years, shall we? In January 1954, the world's first nuclear submarine, the Nautilus, was launched from the shipyards in Groton, Connecticut. Boasting a crew of 105, it was the first ship to cruise beneath the North Pole's polar ice cap. The Nautilus is on display today at Groton's Submarine Museum.

Okay, let's zip ahead again. On November 23, 2004, the United States launched the U.S.S. Jimmy Carter, the nation's newest nuclear attack submarine from the place of its origin – Groton, Connecticut. It has a contingent of 133, and the firepower is awesome. We've come a long way in an awfully short time!

The U.S. Navy Submarine Force Museum in Groton is a great place to visit and to appreciate the challenging work of the men and women in the silent service. The museum is owned and operated by the navy and is not lacking for materials to peruse. There are thousands upon thousands of artifacts, documents and photographs for the public to explore while touring the facility.

The museum is open throughout the year and offers several dynamic events to which the public is invited. Added to these is the public's ability to explore several submarines which are, or have been, active in service to the country. There is a terrific store on the grounds if one would like to purchase a nautical keepsake of the visit.

Haven't had enough of the sea? Take a short drive over to the Coast Guard Training Station in Groton. The facility has a history dating back to the Revolutionary War and is the site of the Battle of Groton Heights. It was a gory affair; and no matter whose account one reads, it was not a glorious day for either the Americans or the British.

Groton has recently celebrated its 300th anniversary. It has a tradition of, by and for the sea. The motto of this steadfast community is simply, "Past, Present and Future." Simply put, Groton is a city to visit, and a city to appreciate.

THE NEW ENGLAND AQUARIUM

If you like fish, I mean really like fish, the New England Aquarium is a must for you. The folks there do like their fish in a big way!

Some folks have fish bowls in their reception areas. Others have tanks in their bedrooms. Some have aquariums in their living rooms. Some of those are fairly good-sized, too. But, if you like fish, I mean really like fish, the New England Aquarium is a must for you. The folks there do like their fish in a big way!

To begin, once you're inside, you are looking at a 200,000 gallon aquarium!

"Billy, you wanted that aquarium. Now, you're going to have to clean it."

"Aww, mom."

The tank has everything inside from very large and very predatory sharks, to some magnificent sea turtles, and from stingrays to moray eels. The place does have some frightening-looking fish, but that's what life is like under the waves not so many yards away. There are some 15,000 living critters within the confines of the NEA.

The place is enormous and busy, and it has been busy since it opened its doors in 1969. Some 12,000 people visited on the opening day, and the crowds haven't stopped coming since.

There is a poisonous fish tank and a "touch 'em" tank for the kids (not the same tank). The life inside the glass is a treat to observe and will thrill young and old alike. And, if you like your fish at an even safer distance, you may want to check them out on the IMAX screen also inside the building.

I become a kid again when I visit there (although I wasn't a kid in '69). I am awed by the colors of the fish and the majesty of the giant beasts. I am amazed that so many creatures are swimming right before my eyes in a tank several stories high. I suppose a little part of my brain wonders, "What would happen if there were one little crack right down there at the bottom? Naaah, that's not going to happen."

My particular favorite part of the expedition is watching the divers feed the sharks. They do this twice a day. Whatever it is that these folks get paid, it's not nearly enough!

A visit there doesn't have to be totally indoors. For a few dollars more, a visitor can take a boat from the dock and go whale watching. These large beauties seem to be waiting just off the coast to have their pictures taken.

The NEA is definitely an eye-popper. There is so much to take in. Oh, and make sure to take in the gift shop. The souvenirs are certainly worth having, and the prices aren't fishy!

WINE COUNTRY - NEW ENGLAND

Contrary to popular belief, New England is very well-suited for grape-growing. Many varieties of grapes do well in temperatures as low as 29 degrees below zero.

When most folks think wine, they may muse about the richness of California's Napa Valley, or the earthy wonders of Italy's Asti region, or the sensual delights of the Bordeaux region of France. Well, wine lovers, you just may want to hop in the ol' family car and check out the truly-amazing wineries of New England.

Not that many years ago, one might have been hard put to locate a single wine-producing vineyard. Oh, sure, the region had mills and factories in abundance, but you just couldn't savor the fine smoky texture of a mellow cordovan shoe, or the fruity headiness of roll of wire.

By the end of the twentieth century, the factory era in the Northeast was virtually over. Conversely, the wine era was just beginning. (Coincidence? Hmmm.) But, wine in New England is not just a recent fad. Let's face it, the Vikings arrived here about 1,000 A.D., and they really weren't teetotalers. In fact, they actually christened this new country "Vinland" (land of wine).

All these many years, grape growing for wine production was more or less a cottage industry. Folks, my grandparents included, worked small plots of land in the hills of Worcester to grow grapes. And, I have a pretty good hunch that those home-corked jugs of wine sold to discerning local wine fanciers managed to get my immigrant family through the rough years of the Great Depression.

But, why the sudden interest in developing award-winning regional wines? Well, besides the fact that the mills have, for the most part, closed. Farming is not as common a practice as it once was. Transportation has improved to facilitate travel to the more rural expanses of the greater Northeast. Folks today have more expendable cash, And, probably most importantly, developments in the agrisciences have fostered strains of hearty grapes that are simply perfect for the area.

Contrary to popular belief, New England is very well-suited for grape-growing. Many varieties of grapes do well in temperatures as low as 29 degrees below zero. (They just may not thrive in summer's heat, however.) New England's soil is rich and nearly perfect for good growth patterns. It's hilly in the Northeast (No kidding!), and, again, perfect for drainage and irrigation. Keep in mind, boggy meadows don't allow for good grape growth. If you have five years on your hands, you can begin to foster a tradition of great vines that are almost certain to be wonderful grape producers.

Just how popular is the new interest in wine. I would say, "Business is booming!" Presently, in New England, there are some 101 wineries. That truly is an amazing growth pattern. Keep in mind, I'm talking here solely about the wine industry. The region is also experiencing a powerful interest in beer and spirits. By the way, that old Viking staple, mead, is also making a terrific comeback with those who consider a slight imbibition to be a sampling of the nectar of the gods.

In recent years, Child Bride and I have discovered and rediscovered some very delightful wineries in south central region. In fact, twice we have been privileged to be members of the harvest crew at the Flag Hill Winery in Lee, New Hampshire. If you've never experienced a grape harvest, you are truly missing out on a magnificent treat. (My wife's favorite part was getting to stomp grapes.)

My recommendation is to clear adequate space in the trunk of your roadster; pack your beloved into the front seat, and set out on a New England wine adventure. You don't have to thank me for the advice; but if you're in the neighborhood, you could simply drop off a bottle of cabernet sauvignon. I wouldn't mind at all.

A SIGN OF THE TIMES

*Hand-carved wooden signs are simply
a part of New England life.*

You see them nearly everywhere in New England. They grace the fronts of small shops. They dangle on metal braces in front of bar rooms. They stand on wooden pillars on the lawns of dentists' offices, and are identical on both sides. They're in large cities, small towns, seaside communities and mountain resort areas. Hand-carved wooden signs are simply a part of New England life.

They are the part of region's life which returns New Englanders back to our colonial roots. They are substantial and generally quite unassuming. They touch us to our core without us really knowing why.

The art of wood carving, more specifically, sign carving isn't dead. Lots of folks, men and women alike, have the tools of the trade down in their cellars or in their garage workshops. Usually, they are proud to display the dings, divots and scars they sustained while fashioning a name plate for their Cape Cod or their bungalow. More often than not, they're delighted to craft out a sign or symbol for a neighbor or a relative as a gift or upon request. Generally, it is that sign which is found among the most treasured items of that individual.

Is it the feel of them? The texture of carved wood smoothed by fine sandpaper? Is it the colors? They are usually bright basic colors applied in short, measured strokes. Is it the subject matter . . . a sailboat on a sunlit morning, a pheasant in flight, or a mountain vista. Anything or everything about them is an anchor to our New England way of life.

"That's old Doc Fletcher's place over there. He's the local vet. See that sleepy bulldog next to that tabby cat on his sign? He's been here since '76."

"Across the street over there, that's Johnson Real Estate. You know it's his place. He's got that colonial carved in his sign. It's an exact replica of his house."

"Oh, yes, and over here is Williams' Antique Shop. It's the fourth generation of our family now. See that oil lamp carved in the sign? Jeb Williams hung that on his porch when he used to trade antiques out of the back of his wagon nearly one hundred years ago."

And some of the better taverns (so I'm told) just don't have their signs on the outer walls, they grace so many of the walls and ledges throughout the establishments. Ancient plaques of men's boxing clubs from the turn of the century; nameplates of old New England whaling ships and signs from long-extinct trucking companies, welcome signs to towns in Cape Cod, and so much more help to ease the patron into a blissful and nostalgic frame of mind.

New England is a region steeped in tradition. Generation after generation adds its knowledge and experiences to the substance of the preceding ones. It's a building process, but every good builder knows that you just don't toss out the old for something new. Hand-carved New England signs just may be one of the facets of life in this fair region which gives substance and stability to a wonderful way of life. Oh, for the record, the vast neon of Las Vegas is not allowed.

MELLOW IN THE BERKSHIRES

*There is no place, absolutely no place, better to relax
and enjoy the moment better than at a concert under
the stars in Tanglewood.*

Summer in New England is a reward. Folks have done all that they can to restore and fortify their castles from the rigors of the last two seasons and feel they can do no more in preparation for the seasons yet to come. It is time to relax and enjoy the present. There is no place, absolutely no place, better to relax and enjoy the moment better than at a concert under the stars in Tanglewood.

I enjoy music. I love to hear every note in a piece. If it is to be played, I want to hear it. (Child Bride wishes I would be as enraptured by all that she has to say. Alas, I try.) This why I chose to address Tanglewood's acoustics first and foremost. They are spectacular . . . A-1 . . . outstanding! A devotee of any form of the musical arts could not find a better place (my humble subjective opinion) on the planet to appreciate anything melodious than here in Massachusetts' Berkshires. Acoustics experts have tried to capture the essence of the sound production in other concert venues throughout the world. Tanglewood appears to be the gold standard by which concert musical quality is measured.

Tanglewood made its appearance on the music scene in 1936, opening up to a crowd of 15,000. Word must have spread like wildfire, because at least one-third of a million music lovers now pack the arena annually. The Boston Symphony (BSO) played that first year. They were so well received , that "The Shed" was opened the following year to house them.

The grounds cover over 200 acres, but there are only seats for some 5,000 fans up close and personal with the performers. That's not a problem for most folks, because that still leaves plenty of room to spread out a blanket; kick off the sandals; light the candleabras; drop a lobster or two into a pot; pop the cork on a great wine; and listen to the stars under the stars. And the stars (the ones on stage) run the gamut from the best in classical to dance, and from theater to pop. If you can't find something to enjoy there, you just ain't tryin'.

Folks, I'm not going to tell you all you need to know about Tanglewood. That's why we have the internet! (Cyberspace is your friend. Embrace it.) There are terrific facilities in which to dine and lodge when you're in the Berskhires. There are also a myriad of things to do in the region beyond the music; it's impossible not to have a great time there.

Gentle Reader with your indulgence, I would like to share a personal moment here. Thank you. I was driving along the Mass Pike one evening so many years ago. I had the windows down and was simply enjoying air whistling through the car. Suddenly, I began to hear a wonderful piece of music. As I continued eastward, I slowed, and the music became louder. I began to notice cars parked along the shoulder of the highway. The piece being played was the Boston Pops rendition of Tchaikovsky's "1812 Overture." The music built to a crescendo, and then the cannons blasted and the church bells peeled.

There must have been several hundred of us parked against the berm of the Pike crying and cheering like fools. I don't recommend listening to concerts at Tanglwood from the side of the road. I do, however, recommend catching a concert, any concert, or two . . . or three . . . or ten!

MOOSE ALLEY

Moose Alley, is just outside of Pittsburg, NH and just south of the Canadian border. It's a dozen-mile stretch of magnificent creatures with amazing racks.

How do you like your moose . . . large . . . up close . . . plentiful? Yes, I thought so . . . all of the above. That being the case, I've got just the place for you to visit . . . Moose Alley is just outside of Pittsburg, NH, and just south of the Canadian border. It's a dozen-mile stretch of magnificent creatures with amazing racks . . . hey, I'm talking about antlers!

I know what you're thinking. You're saying to yourself, "Yeah, what if I get there and no one's home?" "What if the entire moose population decided to take a hike into Canada?" The answer to both of those questions is, "Not going to happen!"

Allow me to give you an example of just how plentiful the Bullwinkles are.

My wife and I spotted a large male along the side of the road in a clearing. He was directly in front of us, looking both ambivalent and majestic. I was in the process of trying to adjust my camera for the optimal shot, when Child Bride suddenly went into panic mode.

"Drive! Drive! He's trying to get into the car," she screamed.

"What are you talking about," I said, watching the blissful animal two feet from the headlights. He could care less about us."

"Not that one," she said, almost crawling up on my lap, "THIS ONE!"

At that moment, a Bullwinkle clone was in the process of pushing his massive snout into the open passenger window. I'm certain he was trying to give my wife a large, northern New Hampshire smackeroo. I'm not sure of this, but I think I saw moose tears in my rearview mirror.

People will tell you the best times to see moose are at dusk and dawn, because these animals are crepuscular. That's not completely true. Many moose seem intent in breaking that stereotype and meander across roads and fields at all hours of the day and night.

Locals may want to sell you moose callers. My wife wasn't doing anything but sitting. Those big fellas will saunter right up to you, whether you're calling or not.

Locals may not tell you not to get too up-close-and-personal with moose, but I'm telling you. Don't do it! Moose are very large animals with antlers. You are visiting them in their backyards and they will graciously treat you as a guest as long as you don't decide to get too chummy with them. There will be: NO PETTING! NO FEEDING! And, absolutely NO TEASING! Oh, and leave the dog back at your log cabin retreat. Squirrels play well with moose. Dogs don't!

NEW ENGLANDERS
MAKE GOOD NEIGHBORS

It is a common practice in this region not only to welcome a new neighbor with a plate of goodies or a potted plant, but to let the new folks know if the need arises they will be more than just "ol' what's-his-name next door," Neighbors get involved.

Robert Frost said, "Good fences make good neighbors." That may be true, but New Englanders don't need fences or stonewalls to be neighborly; we just are. Let's face it, the Magnificent Realm of the Northeast is not that large (slightly more than one-third the size of Texas). Additionally, the weather and some terrain in the region can be a little less than hospitable. We know this to be true, and we go on with our lives.

I'm not saying that the weather and the land help to create wonderful neighbors. What may be true is that trying conditions may help to bring out the best in us . . . our neighborliness. On those rare occasions when a motorist slides into a ditch during a storm, or the Atlantic hurls a bolder into the side of a car, several new Englanders (strangers, but neighbors nonetheless) will make their way through the storm to do all that they can to assist. And, yes, it's true, we even help New Yorkers when they are stranded and need assistance. (The only possible exception might be outside of Fenway Park.)

The folks we see, or don't see, who live around us, are terrific examples of great neighbors. They may not pop over daily to let you know they are there, but they ARE there. It is a common practice in this region not only to welcome a new neighbor with a plate of goodies or a potted plant, but to let the new folks know if the need arises they will be more than just "ol' what's-his-name next door." Neighbors get involved.

New Englanders who have strayed to other states may find it difficult to understand they don't know the people only a few yards away. They may see them. They may even wave to them, but those folks just don't open themselves to being neighbors. (It could be that they mistake us for New Yorkers, but that's just my guess.)

New England folk visit. They drop unexpected plates of food on your doorstep. They give you their key when they go on vacation. They watch out for your dog. They pitch in to help you dig out from a nor'easter. The men on the street on which I lived in Worcester had a standing rule: If a snowstorm packed more than a six-inch wallop, they would meet at the corner store. From that point, they would dig out the street for an entire block! After it was done, they would get together with their wives to celebrate. Now, those are what I call neighbors.

No, the stories about New Englanders being standoffish are definitely myths. We understand all too well that we are all in this life together. We know what it is to go through the rigors of a long, hard winter; and we certainly know what it is to savor each cool summer evening . . . on a front porch . . . with a laugh . . . over a glass of lemonade. Oh, the joys of New England living!

CABIN FEVER

Then, the first snow comes in. New Englanders bundle up and bound outside. They attack the walk with a vengeance. They build snowmen. They throw a sled in the back of the car and take the kids to the nearest hill. Then, the second storm hits.

New Englanders are tough. Any arguments? I didn't think so. And, a little snow storm is not about to addle the brains of the folk from the majestic northern regions of America's Atlantic coast, right? You bet. But, what about the second, third and tenth? Well, maybe . . . just a little. After all, we're only human.

Beginning before Halloween, the folks from the region begin to pack it in. The sun's not coming back for a while, so the lawn chairs go to the basement,the lawnmower goes to the shed, the screens come down, and the storm windows go up. A little extra food is added to each shopping trip. The snow tires are dusted off and mounted. You get the picture.

Then, the first snow comes in. New Englanders bundle up and bound outside. They attack the walk with a vengeance. They build snowmen. They throw a sled in the back of the car and take the kids to the nearest hill. Then, the second storm hits.

The walks are a little narrower. The snowman is patched up. And, the hill can take care of itself.

By the time winter has reached double digit storm, not a lot of folk are bundled up and bounding. They're listening to the wind blow. They're cursing out the Weather Channel. They're drawing pictures of the sun and pasting them on the refrigerator. They're hunkering! To hunker means "to squat or take a task seriously." New Englanders do both during winter. Nearly every home has a war chest of board games that reappear year after year when the first snowflakes touch the ground. They do 'em all. They hold family tournaments. (Loser shovels the walk.)

The arts and crafts are brought out. This is a great pastime. The old teach the young. The kids develop a true appreciation for grandma when they're sitting over a cup of hot chocolate, and she's teaching them how to 'knit one and pearl two.'

Snow days make for serious home time. The schools are shut down. (If you listen very closely, you may hear every parent mutter something unkind when the radio announcements are given.) Roads may be impassable. Malls don't open. New England battens down. What do the folk do? They cope.

It is amazing how many pastries are created in the winter months. The aromas are delicious, and everyone is involved. The fruits, which were canned in the fall, become the pie made in February.

"Creative" is the operative word to handle winter in the northern climes. Let's face it, there's only so much sleeping a person can do. Families have in-house fashion shows. They make watching a video a "theatrical experience." And, they do lots of letter writing to people who are less fortunate and live outside of New England.

Couples are careful not to tread too closely to one another as February turns into March. When a trip to the half-buried mailbox seems like a trek through the frozen tundra, folks tend to try to be loving yet brief in their encounters with their mates. Creativity here is of the essence as well.

Nothing says, "I love you, and we'll get through this together" like some homemade gift placed on a pillow . . . a cup of tea brought to the significant other when he or she is deep into a book (or after a long, arduous war with the shovel) . . . a ribbon leading from the door to a hot, scented bath. Throw in a deep back massage, and you've amassed 1,000 bonus points). I know, a little squishy, right?

Then, just when you think you've run out of ideas and patience . . . a crocus is blooming in your window box. It's Red Sox pre-season. Fishing season begins tomorrow! The snowbirds next door have returned. You're airing out your camp and hoping that you'll fit in last year's swimsuit.

THE HOMES OF NEW ENGLAND

What the area has is character . . .
lots and lots of character.

By anyone's standards, the New England states form a compact confederation. They're nearly pieced together and wedged into a corner of the United States, away from the ebb and flo of the rest of the country. I've been in most of the other states and lived in several of them. I'm delighted to say it, "I'm back!"

I've been trying to put my finger on some of what is unique about this region, and it occurred to me that housing and how that housing is laid out is quite unlike most regions of the country. That may be a statement of broad simplification, but the diversity of structures in New England may be one of our more endearing qualities.

Certainly, the area has stayed current with condos, split levels, and ranch-styled homes. Sprinkled here and there are a few geodesic domes, solar-powered wigwams or a refurbished school bus on pontoons (which may cause you to get whiplash is you're driving by them); but they are few and far between. What the area has is character . . . lots and lots of character.

Some urban areas have mile after mile of "three deckers." They are three-family houses which began sprouting up in the late 1870's. They were built near factories and were the first homes that many immigrant families knew. They were great for housing lots of kids who liked to play street football and baseball. I know. I grew up in one.

Large Victorian homes grace the landscape in many cities as well. They certainly have not lost their charm over the years. Their stately presence adds a sort of somber tranquility to any and all neighborhoods.

Mill towns are found near rivers and streams. In and around these areas are long row houses . . . the original town houses. These homes stand side by side and share outer walls to separate them from one another.

In rural regions, not very far from many towns are some magnificent "telescope" homes. In years past, a couple would build a sizable house. When the kids grew up and married, they didn't leave home. They inherited the large unit, and the older generation moved into a smaller unit attached to the first. This process sometimes went on for four or five generations. Family reunions were never a problem here.

A similar type of structure is found in some of the more rural areas. These folks apparently didn't believe in "out buildings." All of the buildings, i.e., the barn, the storage shed, the summer kitchen and mother-in-law abode are all attached or connected with enclosed above-ground tunnels. A guy could hide from his wife for weeks at a time and never leave home!

Along the coast, there are more than a few Cape Codders, garrisons and ancient captain's homes. Those come complete with widow's walk roofs.

There are homes that go back to the late 1600's. There are rambling colonial homes . . . the real things. Some owners will proudly point out a musket ball hole or a pair of initials probably carved by the original owner's child. (I wonder if the original owner was covered for that kind of damage.) There are schools, train stations, factories and what-have-you which have become new residences and still retain the charm of their original style.

And, in Hampton, New Hampshire, there's a small park with several very old New England farm houses surrounding it. When somebody wasn't looking about 1905, a Sears home sprung up right next to them. It's a small home . . . a beautifully quaint home that fits very well in New England. It's the home that Child Bride and I call our own, and we're very happy here.

HOW'S THAT AGAIN?

*Those from this, the wonderful region
in the country, who have traveled the rest of our fair land
have been easily identified as 'feriners' because of
what we say and how we say it.*

The wind howled across some of the nastiest terrain in the southwest. Sand caked my car windows and caused my engine to cough and sputter. Ah, a dim light just off to the side of the road. Slim's Café. What luck! I tilted my head into the wind and pulled my hat low over my eyes. I dragged myself to the front door. I put my shoulder to the door to work it open. Then, I had to shove it doubly hard to close it once again. The waiter was gruff-looking and had a definite need of a shave. There was a wizened character at the bar nursing a cup of coffee. They turned to look at me.

"The sand seems to be killing my engine," I said, using my hat to dust off my jeans. "And, I really could use a root beer or any kind of cold tonic."

There was a groove between the counterman's eyes, and a dime could have stood there at attention. The customer turned to me and gave me his full consideration. His Stetson was pushed back on his silver hair. He worked a toothpick to the corner of his mouth and growled, "So, what part of Massachusetts are you from?"

"Worcester," I said incredulously. "Main South Worcester."

"S'at so," he said, scratching his chin with a matchbook. "My sister still lives in Main South. You wouldn't happen to know a . . ."

So it goes. Those from this, the wonderful region in the country, who have traveled the rest of our fair land, have been easily identified as 'feriners' because of what we say and how we say it. I suppose it's true. We do tend to drop our terminal "r's." We turn them into "ahs." We also tend to stick those dang "r's" onto words that in end an "ah" sound to come up with something like "Havaner, Cuber makes good cigahs." In my 30+ year jaunt around the country, I have seen myself somewhat as The Messenger of the Correctly Spoken Word." Everyone I met, however, thought I had a severe speech impediment.

New Englanders have maintained some terms which are unique to this region. For the novice, a water fountain (the kind you drink from) is a "bub-blah." A soda (Coke, Pepsi, or any soft drink) is a "tonic." Sauce on pasta is gravy. Bags are sacks (unless they are full of potatoes). Shopping carts are carriages, and purses are pocketbooks. Service rendered by anyone is clearly punctuated by "All set?" (What else would fit the occasion . . . Set, ready, go!)

I've also been told that New Englanders speak way to quickly. We're aware of that. We speak rapidly as a life-saving service to the listener. You see, we are aware that this cooler clime has a negative effect on some folks, i.e., freezing to death; and we certainly wouldn't want that to happen when we're trying to give directions to the closest antique store. My thought on the matter is that we may not speak faster than others in the country; we simply listen quicker.

Another characteristic of New England speech is that we tend to be nasal. This certainly can't be true. I've spoken to thousands of my fellow citizens from this fair region, and no one seems to have a sinus condition. We speak so well, in fact, that I contend we have some of the best romantic speakers in the Western world living right here. Can you imagine the look of sheer joy on a girl's face when she would hear the words, "I love ya, Mariarrr. Let's take the cah and head to Savannarrr for a bananarrr. Eh, sweethaht?" Who could resist that lover, right?

Ah, New England, come up and learn the language of love . . . right afta we pahk ya cah in hahvid yahd. All set?

TALKING TURKEY –
NEW ENGLAND STYLE

"Tom turkey. There's a big tom turkey in the front yard."

I stayed up late the evening and watched the Red Sox lose in extra innings. It was tough to get to sleep after that, and nearly impossible to raise my head from the pillow the next morning until . . .

Child Bride called excitedly from downstairs. Coming out of a deep sleep, I heard, "Big Tom Murphy is standing in the yard!"

I rose from bed, threw on a robe, fumbled down stairs and called back; "Who's Tom Murphy, and what is he doing in the yard?"

She looked at me as though my head had suddenly sprouted mold. She then closed her eyes, pointed out the front window and enunciated very clearly, "Tom turkey. There's a big tom turkey in the front yard.'

She was only one-third correct. There was a huge tom in our front yard, but there were also two very well-fed females as well.

For the record, I've seen wild turkeys, but never up close and personal and certainly not for an extended period of time. Further, I never remember seeing a wild turkey in the area when I was younger. It appears I was correct in my observation.

Back at the time our Puritan forefathers took up residence in the area, the landscape was thick with turkeys. Some two centuries later, the great birds were virtually hunted out of existence. Quite a shame if you consider Ben Franklin proposed that the wild turkey should be our national bird. After all, it was readily available throughout the known United States, and it was good to eat! His choice lost to the Bald Eagle by only one congressional vote.

Population growth, infringement on natural habitat and use of chemicals didn't endear the scarce number of birds to the region. It was all but gone.

In the late 1960's, attempts were made in the region to introduce domesticated turkeys into the wild. The plan failed miserably. In 1975, some 25 wild turkeys from New York were reintroduced into New England. Apparently, they liked what they found. Best estimates are that some 25,000 birds are year-round residents in the southern half of the Granite State today.

In case you've only seen the bird on a Thanksgiving table, you may not recognize them in their dress clothes. The males are more colorful than the females. They have blue heads and bright red wattles. They have dark iridescent feathers and a long breast tassel. They are about 3½ to 4 feet in length (although the tom in my yard was certainly much larger). The females have blue-gray heads, lack wattles and are less iridescent.

The birds are not tremendous fliers. They are, however, great walkers and cover fairly-sizable distances on foot at a fairly rapid clip.

The birds nest on the ground. They usually lay about a dozen buff-colored eggs at a time. Ironically, the birds sleep in tall trees. A word to the wise: watch out for my friend Tom after dark. Those topmost branches may not be all that sturdy.

Hunting season is just around the corner. Please keep in mind, our president does pardon a bird or two each year .

THE JIMMY FUND

12-year old cancer patient, Jimmy. He was a Braves fan.
Listeners were requested to send in whatever they could in
hopes $20,000 could be raised for the boy's medical care.
Listeners didn't send in $20,000; they sent in over ten times
that amount! That was the birth of the Jimmy Fund.

Child Bride, a non-native New Englander, and I, a home grown, went to a movie recently. After the previews, there was a short announcement on the Jimmy Fund. It was followed by a can being passed around the audience. Child Bride wore an incredulous expression, while I tugged at my wallet.

"What's the Jimmy Fund," she asked.

"The Jimmy Fund? You don't know?" Now it was my turn to wear an incredulous expression. Then the light bulb over my head shone brightly. "That's right. You're not from around here!"

Child Bride's look showed borderline tolerance; not much more.

"I'm sorry. Really. I guess I just assumed everyone knows of the Jimmy Fund. Well, let me tell you."

Child Bride sat on the edge of her seat expecting a short answer. She wasn't getting one.

"The Jimmy Fund began in 1948 in Boston, when the Hub City was the home for the Braves as well as the Red Sox. During that year, the nationally-aired radio show, Variety Club, teamed up with the Braves to give one very memorable night to a 12-year old cancer patient, Jimmy. He was a Braves fan, and the team crowded into his hospital room where they all sang Take Me Out to the Ball Game. Listeners were requested to send in whatever they could in hopes $20,000 could be raised for the boy's medical care and perhaps to buy him a television, so he could watch his team. Listeners didn't send in $20,000; they sent in over ten times that amount! That was the birth of the Jimmy Fund.

"I don't believe that there are more than a handful of New Englanders, and now there is one less, who haven't heard of the Jimmy Fund. It does terrific work in attempting to find a cure for cancer in children, and they have been at it for over 50 years now."

"In 1953, The Jimmy Fund teamed up with the Boston Red Sox after the Braves moved to Milwaukee. To add more fuel to the Jimmy fund endeavors, the Massachusetts Chiefs of Police named the Jimmy Fund is its charity of the year."

"Through the years, quality people and organizations have espoused the Jimmy Fund and have worked to find the cure. There was the Pan-Massachusetts Bike Challenge in 1980. In 1983, the Jimmy Fund Golf Program was organized. The Boston Marathon folks got involved in 1989, and Stop & Shop worked to raise one million dollars for the campaign in 1991."

"Here's the big news. The original Jimmy was really a fellow named Einar Gustafson. He returned to Dana Farber in 1998 to lend his name to the causes of the Jimmy Fund. The man truly had been a success story. The work of the Braves and the Jimmy Fund had paid off. Mr. Gustafson died in 2001 at the age of 65., Sooo, how about some pop corn to go along with the movie?"

Child Bride looked at me as though I had turned scaly green. The look of borderline tolerance had returned.

"You've got to be kidding," she said in a growl. "Forget the popcorn. We don't need it. What we do need is to make another contribution to the Jimmy Fund. Now, march yourself out to the lobby and do it!"

I did.

TAKE PRIDE IN
YOUR BASEMENTS

Men of New England are particularly
proud of one item . . . their basements.

Lots of people are proud of their possessions. Most are proud of their clothes. Many are proud of their collections of antiques, quilts, stamps or what have you. Men of New England are particularly proud of one item . . . their basements.

For those of you who don't know, a basement is a rather more ornate version of a cellar. In yesteryear, those places were dark and dingy. Many had dirt floors, and most contained the tools needed to keep up the yard or make repairs around the house. My not-so-fondest memories include my nightly wintertime excursions down to the bowels of the cellar from my third floor tenement residence in Worcester. My chore was to haul up ten gallon glass bottles of oil to burn for fuel. Perhaps this is the reason I've always thought of myself as a summer kind of guy.

Time passed, and people started to add light to those dungeons. Somebody thought it would be a marvelous idea to put real floors on the dirt, and the rush was on. Soon, people put a splash of paint here and a shelf there.

My guess is that it was about the point when some guy in Shrewsbury dragged a dart board below ground that women became involved. They weren't going to let the men have all of the fun. Besides, it was another room to refurbish.

"Honey, I was thinking that this large picture of my mother would look terrific in the center of that wall."

"Dear, don't you remember that is where my bar was going to go. I was thinking over there in the corner behind the furnace would be just great."

No one said that finishing off a basement moved forward without skirmishes. The guys really wanted to claim the subterranean area as their own. Who knows? Maybe the basement is the last great link to our cave-dwelling past . . . place for the men of the tribe to gather and bond . . . to exchange stories of great hunts . . . to tell tales of horrible storms from seasons past . . . a place to play poker!

Invariably, when one New England couple visits another, the woman of the house will take the visiting lady to her needlepoint, the breakfast nook or to her collection of fine linen in the cedar chest. The visiting man is nearly always taken to the lowest level of the house. Personally, I have seen more basements than a retiring plumber. I recall my last visit to the nether regions.

"Yep, I got my pool table ordered. It will go over there. I got my 42" plasma to go here. My reading lamp will go over my Lazy Boy and my hot tub will go right over here."

"How great," I exclaimed. My eyes were dancing in my head. This guy had a true male Disneyland just beneath his kitchen.

Finishing my visit with one of the greatest members of the male tribe, I turned to Child Bride and began to state my plan as tactfully as possible.

"Sweets, when I was down in Harry's basement . . . "

"Oh yes, did he tell you that Harriet has plans to turn it into her sewing room? She's going to have all of the girls over there every Wednesday to make curtains and things just like on the Home and Garden Channel. She's going to move all of his things up into the attic."

There's nothing like it. New England men enjoying pool in the attic . . . ducking under a pitched roof . . . hunching over a bar . . . playing darts on their knees . . . and watching the big game while lying on the floor breathing in the sweet smell of insulation. The attic . . . it's definitely a place where the true men of the Northeast can go to get away from it all.

MARKING THE TERRITORY

*But, by God, it's their land! (At least for a day or two after a
snowstorm . . . or until they get a ticket . . . or the garbage
truck rolls around . . . or worse).*

The folks of Boston and Worcester, Massachusetts are very territorial about
their little plots of land. I am speaking here of the land on the street, next to
the curb, that is under their parked cars. They own no deed to the spot. They
didn't purchase it from anyone. They haven't enacted personal cases of emi-
nent domain. But, by God, it's their land! (At least for a day or two after a
snowstorm . . . or until they get a ticket . . . or the garbage truck rolls around
. . . or worse).

There was a certain protocol to this grab. First, the deeper the snow, the
The folks in these parts began a tradition long ago by marking the spots
they shoveled out with some old personal possessions: ironing boards, kitch-
en chairs, bookcases, an end table or two or sawhorses and such could be
easily found during the days following storms marking "ownership" of said
spots by the folks who shoveled them. Until recently, there had been no leg-
islation against this winter ritual; it was simply understood that the act of
shoveling out a vehicle entitled that individual to that spot until the Red Sox
home opener.

There was a certain protocol to this grab. First, the deeper the snow, the
more fiercely the spot was protected. A husband would leave for work in the
morning and move a floor lamp or foot locker into the spot. The wife was
then expected to work all of her chores around the window closest to the spot
to fend off any would-be parkers. Threats of violence and flying objects were
frequently considered to be fair game.

An exception to this pirate parking was when company called next door.
Everyone has company. Most company comes in cars. So, where is the com-
pany supposed to park? Of course . . . in the spot marked with the bureau.
This became a true test of how much you liked your neighbor.

The visitor would come under the watchful glare of the shoveler's wife
and would give a sheepish smile. The wife would angrily stare at the car
and the neighbor's house from the front door left ajar. Subtle hints . . . oh
yea, you bet. Now, God forbid that the visit continued after the old man left
work. Words and more would be exchanged right there on the streets. Other
neighbors in these packed communities loved this entertainment . . . a great

diversion from cabin fever.

Next, 'thou shall not steal thy neighbor's battered settee.' The reader must understand that this region is highly populated by college students. Students are generally poor folk in need of cheap furnishings, and what could be cheaper than 'free?' No matter how intelligent the students may be, they never seemed to understand that block after block of household goods was not an open-air thrift store. Nothing is more colorful than the language used when a spot "owner" would return home to find grandma's treasured rocker gone! Antique dealers loved winters. They were usually one step ahead of the students . . . and with a big truck, too!

Neighborhood kids would have great fun rearranging the furniture. Moving O'Malley's desk for Pisotti's love seat usually caused all kinds of turmoil when the owners would arrive home. Pisotti would shout, "You wanted my space 'cause I shoveled it better!" O'Malley would scream back, "Yeah, and you took my space 'cause I'm on the corner." The kids would fall over themselves peering from a third floor window.

Those days are seemingly gone now. New laws have placed time constraints on furniture-marked spaces. Old traditions die hard, however. Keep your visits short, and be out of that space before the old man gets home!

COVERED BRIDGES

The nickname for covered bridges in this region is
"kissing bridges" or "courting bridges," because they
are nestled in such romantic locations.

There are over 200 covered bridges throughout New England, but I'm not going to tell you where they are. You're going to have to find them for yourself. Finding them, however, will be well worth your effort. You ask, "Why?" well, this much I'll tell you. The nickname for covered bridges in this region is "kissing bridges" or "courting bridges," because they are nestled in such romantic locations.

Imagine, you and your special someone are trekking along a country road in autumn (okay, you pick the season). You round the bend. There, behind a stand of trees run riot in color and only a few yards to the left of the white church steeple reaching majestically to the heavens, is New England perfection. The bridge spans a babbling brook quite full from recent rains. It is a rough-hewn structure which dates back some two centuries. Just then, a gentle snow begins to fall. You take your true love's hand and you race to the bridge. The two of you are alone . . . just you and the snowflakes. The church bells are chiming softly in the distance. A bushy-tailed squirrel scampers across a stone wall. He has an acorn in his mouth. Your loved one smiles, and you smile back.

That's why we call 'em kissing bridges!

The builders of the early covered bridges didn't have the driver or the horse drawn carriage in mind. Nor was he thinking of the pedestrians . . . or the lovers. He was trying to help keep the rigors of New England from the floorboards of the bridge for as long as possible. Yet, these bridges were built to last. Heavy timber, braced on huge granite blocks was the perfect combination: simple, sturdy and gorgeous. Each one has a severely-pitched roof, designed to keep the snows from building up and collapsing the structure.

Resident and visiting painters and photographers alike traipse the roadsides and riverbeds for just the right angle. Those bridges are magnificent but difficult to capture. You don't want to take your eyes off them. New Hampshire and Vermont have the most bridges. They also have great sunsets and wonderfully panoramic vistas. Take your picnic basket and a blanket. Oh, and don't forget to take the one you love!

THE WICKED WAYS OF
NEW ENGLAND

"Wicked is used to describe everything. There is the
oxymoron variety: "My mom was wicked good to me today.

There's a lot I don't know. I admit that (although not too loudly). One of those select few items is, "How exactly did New England latch onto the word wicked? And, who made it work in just about every conceivable situation? Some think it was a contribution by a presidential candidate who fell short of the mark in the New Hampshire primaries. Others think the word spread throughout the region about the time witches were more popular than MTV. I have my theories, but I would like to know just who the culprit is.

"Wicked is used to describe everything. There is the oxymoron variety: "My mom was wicked good to me today. Something's up." There's irony: "The Yankees? Sure, I wicked love 'em." How about the garden variety euphemism? "It's wicked, wicked cold out there! (The use of the double 'wicked' means a well-digger's derriere doesn't stand a chance.) There's always melodic alliteration: "Well, we had another wonderfully wicked winter in Worcester." This could also be a euphemism, but we all know that winters in Worcester are wicked and wonderful.) Possibly the synecdoche: "Something wicked this way comes." (This, again, probably refers to a winter in Worcester.) The apostrophe also works: "My wicked mother-in-law, God give me strength, is coming down from Orono to visit for a month or two!"

Where the term is used doesn't seem to matter in the fine region of New England. It's a given that 'wicked' will be used in church to designate the truly bad from the rest of us kind and gentle folk. It is possibly more often used in any tavern in which a Bruins' game is on the tube. "Orr just released a wicked slap shot that nearly blew out the netting." It can be found in the classroom at nearly every grade level. "My wicked teacher told us to read War and Peace by next week. (This was actually said in a sixth grade classroom in Montpelier.) It's heard regularly on the five o'clock news and weather report. "Another day of wicked humidity is in store for tomorrow." (When you move your arm quickly and it rains, it's a safe bet that the humidity is fairly wicked.) It is certainly in use on I-90, I-95, I-495 and I-93 and any other road in New England. "Will you wicked put down that wicked cell phone and wicked drive your wicked car, you wicked twit!" (sorry, a personal irk of mine.) And, my fondest use of the word is during the cold and flu season. "Ah ga a wicket cood id ma wicket doze, an ah cahn't get wid a day wicket ding."

If you're visiting New England and don't want to stand out as a tourist, simply and generously sprinkle a few hundred 'wickeds' into your speech. No one will know the difference.

Tourist: Can you wicked tell me how to wicked get to Fenway Park? I'm trying to wicked catch the wicked ballgame.

Gas Station Attendant: Sure. You turn left onto Brookline Ave. It's straight ahead of you.

Tourist: Wicked thanks, man.

Other Customer: Hey, did you see the New York plates on that guy's car?

Gas Station Attendant: Yeah, but you got to give him credit. At least he's wicked tryin'.

THE BEAUTY OF
THE LONG BOATS

This is a person who finds a calm lake (New England has one or two of them) and trots his or her long, lean craft overhead; places it gently in the water.

Sometime in the '70's there was an article in Playboy (I used to buy Playboy strictly for the articles, much as I ate ice cream for the nutritional value.) It was titled, "The Purity of the Long Distance Runner." It was a wonderful piece depicting the solitude and grace of individuals participating in a sport in which runners challenge themselves.

The runners in New England are truly majestic in both solitude and purpose. There is, however, another type of individual. He or she is not unique to the area, but certainly appears to be representative of the spirit of individuality and perseverance. Those seem to be the qualities which best epitomize the region. Those are qualities possessed by the scull racer.

This is not the type of individual who leaves shore in a rowboat with a bottle of wine and a sketch pad . . . not similar to the person who attempts to combine fly fishing and canoeing . . . close, but not the same as those who journey into the drink in a kayak. This is a person who finds a calm lake (New England has one or two of them); and trots his or her long, lean craft overhead; places it gently in the water; and sets off at the highest speed endurable for the length of that body of water.

That person is not concerned with the types of trees which line the shores to merge with foliage of the surrounding forests. He or she is not really cognizant of those who stop to gaze admirably at his or her efforts. (After all, looking backward while going forward is not exactly the way one makes serious contact with another, is it?) The rower is not concerned with the bedlam in the world, the price of gas, or the prospects of the Red Sox in the next season. It essence, the rower puts back to blade and blade to water for the simple exhilaration of rowing.

The destination is set. The mind is cleared. The rhythm becomes established. The motion becomes the art. The artist and the canvas become one.

Folks may spend a moment watching the rower approach. They may marvel as the rower and the craft pass by. They may sigh in wonder as the scull shrinks into the distance, but they do not understand. For they who watch will never be the one who powers the craft.

For the most part, the sculler does not test the body and mind for the sake of records. The motion may or may not be in preparation for races. The only race the sculler may have of concern is the race of life. He or she is singular upon the pond. The competition is a constant fire within the self.

The movement is simple, economical and exquisite. The movement is poetry. Unspoken.

If you enjoy team sculling competition, vast crowds and tons of cheering, you may want to hit the Boston scene in October for the Head of the Charles. It's a ton of fun, but don't forget those earplugs.

SHAKY TIMES IN 1755

The quake, although sizable, was not nearly as devastating as the giant quakes which hit Persia and Portugal that same year.

In 1755, America did not extend much beyond the Alleghany (the correct spelling at the time) River. This country wasn't yet a nation, but it certainly was headed in that direction. The Northeast was filling quickly with British subjects.

The British weren't alone in the northeast. They had been welcomed to the region by Native Americans. The Abnaki, a close relative of the Penobscot, called, "The People of the East," saw the number of European faces grow from a few to several thousand. It might be said that in that year the two groups were attempting the practice of peaceful coexistence. The new residents to the region, however, were about to have a very jarring experience.

Much like the late fall and early winter of 2005, that same period over 250 years ago was very mild indeed. In the pre-dawn hours of Tuesday morning, November 18, the tranquility of the Hampton settlement came to an abrupt end. A violent earthquake shook the region. Although there were no reports of death to any of the inhabitants, there was extensive property damage. Furniture was tossed about; some 1,500 chimneys in the Boston area crumbled, and brick walls locally were split apart. The men aboard a sailing vessel over two hundred miles east of Hampton thought they had hit a rock when the quake occurred. Many scientists believe that the quake could have registered 6.0 or greater in severity.

Some miles away in Greenland, New Hampshire, Captain Samuel Weeks was at rest. He had built a substantial brick house in 1710; it is thought to be the oldest brick house in New Hampshire and is still standing today. It was the 18" beams that saved the house from the quake. So strong were the tremors, however, that all of the beams cracked. The intensity of the jolts, coupled with the reality of the French and Indian War, provided great fodder for Sunday sermons at several area churches.

The quake, although sizable, was not nearly as devastating as the giant quakes which hit Persia and Portugal that same year. Thousands died in each of those quakes. There is a debate as to where exactly the epicenter for the quake that rocked southern the New Hampshire region on that November morning was located. There are indications that the distinctive sand layer found in the Hampton Marsh is consistent with a tsunami deposit from the same time period. If that is true, according to the Re-evaluation of Earthquake Potential and Source in the Vicinity of Newburyport, Massachusetts, it could very well be the "first tsunami recorded along the U.S. Atlantic Seaboard and could point to a source of earthquakes offshore from southeastern New Hampshire and southern Maine.

The earthquake of 1755 was not a fluke. The region does have a history of quakes at least dating back to the Plymouth Colony, in which a sizable quake was recorded in 1638. The quakes were frequent enough that Abnakis had a term for one. Nanamkipoda literally means "when the earth shakes." Another damaging quake occurred on October 29, 1727. The epicenter of this quake was probably located not far from the southeast from Hampton Beach. It caused damage from Boston to Portland, Maine.

With improved seismic testing in the latter part of the 20th century, a line of shakes in the 5.0 to 5.9 range occurred from Bangor, Maine to Philadelphia, Pennsylvania. Some nine quakes were recorded along that line. The liquefaction of soil which occurred in 1727 (and possibly again in 1755) seems to have been centered in the Amesbury, Massachusetts region. This site may be on a yet unidentified fault.

Yes, Hampton, New Hampshire has seen more than a little bit of just about everything Mother Nature has to offer. Many of us can recall a jolt, a blizzard, or a hurricane of some note. All of these events and more help to shape the landscape of the region, and none of them take away from the beauty and livability that the area has to offer.

NEW ENGLAND LIGHTHOUSES

*There are 179 lighthouses in New England, 136 of
which are active. What is a lighthouse? A lighthouse
replaced lightships which guided vessels at sea away from
rocks which New England has in abundance.*

The following story never happened, although many New Englanders swear
it's true. It is a record of radio communications between a U.S. naval ship off
the coast of Maine and another party.

US Ship: Please divert your course 0.5 degrees to the south to avoid a collision.

Reply: Recommend you divert your course 15 degrees to the north to avoid
a collision.

US Ship: This is the captain of a US Navy ship. I say again, divert your
course.

Reply: I say again, you divert YOUR course!

US Ship: THIS IS THE AIRCRAFT CARRIER CORAL SEA! WE ARE
A LARGE WARSHIP OF THE US NAVY. DIVERT YOUR COURSE   NOW!

Reply: This is the West Quoddy Lighthouse Station. Your call!

True or not, you have to admire the spunk and grit of New England lighthouse keepers.

There are 179 lighthouses in New England, 136 of which are active. What
is a lighthouse? A lighthouse replaced lightships which guided vessels at sea
away from rocks, which New England has in abundance. These structures
cast a beam of light (sometimes rotating) miles out to sea. Many a ship's
crew owes its lives to the dedicated folks who have worked the lights during
incredible storms. New England is known to have had a few of those, too.

Technology and improved communications have all but done away with
the need for these magnificent structures. They still provide a much-needed
service to smaller craft nearing the New England shoreline.

21st century innovations don't mean that folks have lost interest in them.
Far from it! The lure of those beauties draws tourists by the thousands to
paint or photograph them in all kinds of weather. You'll easily enough find
folks prowling the rocks or taking tours to catch a glimpse of them. And, the

numbers of lighthouse postcards that are sold is staggering.

Lighthouse restoration groups have taken over the care of many of the structures. These noble groups spend countless hours minding the building with tender loving care to keep them in pristine condition for generations to come.

Maine has the most lighthouses. 68 of them (54 are active) dot the coastline. Interestingly that coastline looks like 228 miles on a map and is actually 3,478 miles, if you count the islands. The Pemaquid Point Light near Bristol is depicted on the Maine state quarter. It was built in 1827 and attracts about 100,000 people each year.

Vermont, yes Vermont, has the least with four and two replicas. Don't forget, there's a fairly-sizable lake bordering Vermont to the west.

For sheer beauty, you can't beat the Nubble Lighthouse in York, Maine the most photographed lighthouse in the world, has also been painted once or twice, also.

And, if you enjoy a majestic seafood dinner, you'll enjoy intimate dining atop the Newburyport Lighthouse, in Newburyport, Massachusetts. The view and the fare are truly second to none.

New England lighthouses are not without their eerie histories. Several generations of folks at the New Castle Lighthouse in southern New Hampshire will testify to seeing the apparition of an ancient lighthouse keeper trudging up the stairs toward the light he dutifully manned for many years. The ghost, however, does not deter many couples from being married next to the beacon.

It all sounds fairly spooky to me . . . the ghost that is, not getting married!

THE RUNNING OF THE BRIDES

This amazing annual event is held in
Filenes's Basement in Boston.

What do you get when you combine the hard-hitting action of the Super Bowl with the Boston Marathon? Simply put, "The Running of the brides." This amazing annual event is held in Filenes's Basement in Boston. Since 1947, future brides have waited outside in the early January morning chill for the doors to be thrown open to take advantage of the tremendous sale on wedding gowns.

"How good is this sale," you ask. Well, it takes a mere 60 seconds for the racks to be stripped bare. The throng of women grab as many gowns as they can and then rush off to convenient corners to try them on. And the prices? The word is that these creations go for about one-fourth of the original price tag. In other words, a $1,000 dress sells for $249!

This is a big league rush, and it's not for the faint of heart. So intense is the frenzy, Filenes's has come out with a few simple suggestions.

First: Leave the men at home. I think that is my favorite. The men tend to slow down these piranhas of purchase. They want to talk when there's buying to be done. Beyond that, men tend to become distracted by women wrenching off their clothing.

Second: Be courteous. Yeah, right! Ladies, the race is won by the swift and the merciless.

Third: Dress for speed. Tennis shoes, sports bras, shorts and quickly-removable tops are recommended. Personally, I would include sharpened elbow pads and a helmet with face masks.

Fourth: Be creative. This usually applies to having an eye for a gown that can be altered to one's personal taste. I see this as an opportunity to bring a friend who is larger than you to run interference, or maybe even act menacingly, so you can scarf up the better items.

Fifth: Be fair. Everyone will most likely get the dress of their dreams. My suggestion is to take serious suggestions two and four.

Sixth: have fun! Ever been checked into the boards in a hockey game? That kind of fun.

Seventh: Don't even think of cutting in front of another woman waiting in line to enter the store. You absolutely don't want to do that!

There are other suggestions for this activity, but they come down to fair play and bonding. Ladies, there are no referees once the doors open. No referees mean no penalties. In football, a team has to forfeit yards for roughing the passer. At this sale, 'roughing the gown-holder' is rewarded by owning the gown.

There are groups or teams of women who dress identically and work as a unit. These precision machines scoop up the gowns, cover the women changing, fend off unwanted hands from the gowns, and move off to the registers with their finds. There are no records kept on how well they do, but best estimates are that these ladies can scavage what they want and be at the nearest bar toasting one another in a matter of minutes.

I guess I have to keep in mind that in a short time following the sale, these gladiators will be the picture of innocence as they slowly make their way down the aisle. Who would have guessed, huh?

Oh, one last suggestion. Ladies, make sure you really like the gown you've snagged. Once you buy it, you own it! There are no returns on these gowns . . . not even if you bring your team.

(The word today is that the Bargain Basement is closing its doors. The hope is the sale will happen again. SOON!)

THE HOWES OF SPENSER

It took Elias a court battle to win the rights he so richly deserved as inventor of the machine, but win it he did.

Route 9 snakes trough central Massachusetts from Boston to Pittsfield. In various sections, the old road is known as "The Ted Williams Highway," "The Old Boston Post Road" and "The United Spanish American War Veteran's Highway. (I've always wanted to give directions by saying, "You take the USAWVH down to The Blarney Stone and take a left. You can't miss it!")

Deep into Worcester County, the town of Spenser straddles Route 9. If you're obeying the speed limit as you meander through the hills of this fair burg, you'll see a sign Howe State Park. After a mere four-mile cruise, you can park in the Dunkin' Donuts parking lot (they really are everywhere), and make your way to a very scenic lake area. It is the former homestead of the Howe family. Judging by the meager remains of the foundation, the family home may not have been much to speak of, but that didn't stop the family from persevering.

Dad owned a saw mill and a grist mill and fathered eight children. Son, Elias, earned a place in a machine shop in Cambridge, which may have been the setting for a brilliant idea . . . the sewing machine. It took Elias a court battle to win the rights he so richly deserved as inventor of the machine, but win it he did.

Elias's brother, William, while helping to build a church in Warren, happened upon an idea for a form of a covered bridge. He had it patented; it is called the Howe Truss Bridge, and it was used extensively by railroad companies throughout the nation.

Not to be denied, Elias's nephew, Tyler, caught the inventing bug and came up with the spring bed. It, too, was patented. To this day, people throughout the world can attribute comfortable nights of sleeping to Tyler's invention.

It should also be noted that Elias received a patent for an "automatic, continuous clothing closure." He didn't seriously try to market it, since he was so involved in the sewing machine. Others did, however; and that invention today is called "the zipper."

THE WRECK OF THE GLENDON

*The Glendon and its crew, however, were no match
for a powerful nor'easter which doomed the ship off
the coast of New Hampshire.*

The Glendon took its proud maiden voyage from Kennybunk, Maine in 1880. It was a large, three-masted schooner and boasted a strong crew of seven. The ship was designed and rigged for heavy loads. In February of 1896, it was laden with 460 tons of coal for destinations in northeastern New England. It never completed its journey.

Keep in mind that 1896 was long before the time when weather bulletins could be issued by the National Weather Service. Doppler radar or enhanced ship-to-shore communication didn't exist. Simply, it was an era when men (sorry, no women on board at this time), braved rough seas on mighty ships. The Glendon and its crew, however, were no match for a powerful nor'easter which doomed the ship off the coast of New Hampshire.

It was mid-afternoon on Sunday, February 9. The gray skies suddenly turned heavy and foreboding. The wind freshened to a gale, bringing with it driving snows. Two schooners worked their way along the coast. One dropped anchor along Salisbury Beach; the other, the Glendon, continued on its coastal trek. It didn't last long in those turbulent waters.

Word was sent to the life saving station at Straw's Point. Soon, help was on the way, but the ferocious storm thwarted efforts to save the crew with the use of a gun firing a line to the stranded men. Time and again, the gun was reloaded and fired. Night fell, but the rescuers did not give up hope. They built a huge bonfire, so that the crew members only a few hundred yards off shore could see that they were not abandoned. The cries for help could be heard over the roar of the ocean.

About 7:00 p.m., another shot was fired and the line did find the rigging. One by one, the crew of the Glendon found his way to it and to safety.

Within a few weeks, approximately 200 tons of coal was salvaged from the Glendon. Later, a portion of the hull was made into a restaurant, which sold chowder and saltwater taffy.

In 1938, veteran fisherman, Albert Dunbrack was tending his lobster traps and found the Glendon's anchor and chain.

Mr. Cutler, the owner of the Sea View House, never wanted to see another disaster such as the wreck of the Glendon. It was through his tireless efforts that a Coast Guard station became a reality at North Beach in Hampton.

The coal in the old of the Glendon was sold to Captain Frank Nudd to be salvaged. It was Nudd who lost his life in the Fourth of July tornado of 1898, but that's another story.

THE TOLLHOUSE COOKIES

Most New Englanders pronounce it, "the
Toll House Cookie" . . . otherwise known as the
chocolate chip cookie. Here's the scoop.

New England can't lay claim to the toll road. There are early Greek references to ferrying the dead across the river Archeron . . . possibly an early form of car-pooling. New England can't stake the cookie as its own. There is some indication that cookies in some form were being munched in seventh-century Persia. After school treats for latch-key kids? Maybe.

Most New Englanders pronounce it "the Toll House Cookie" . . . otherwise known as the chocolate chip cookie. Here's the scoop.

Ruth Wakefield graduated from Framingham State Normal School Department of Household Arts in 1924. After working as a dietician, she and her husband bought the Toll House Restaurant on the outskirts of Whitman, Massachusetts. Built in 1709, the inn was a haven for travelers in eastern Massachusetts. It was a place where the road weary could rest their horses and have a drink before they were once again on their way. It was on that same site some 200 years later that the Wakefields decided to open their lodge, the Toll House Inn.

Ruth made exceptional meals for her guests, and a favored part of each meal was her delicious desserts. On one occasion, she was preparing Butter Drop Do or dough cookies and decided to add some Nestle Semi-Sweet Chocolate to the batch. She expected the chocolate to melt. It didn't. It generally held its shape and nestled in nicely with the rest of the sweet concoction. Voila! Instant hit!

The Boston newspapers picked up the story and the recipe. Other New England newspapers followed suit. Soon, sales of Nestle's Semi-Sweet Chocolate bars took off like a rocket. Industrious woman that she was, Ruth went to Nestle, and soon they were printing her recipe on the side of the package of semi-sweet chocolate. The inevitable happened, and soon the bars became bags of semi-sweet Chocolate Morsels. That was in 1939. Today, the cookies are made and devoured worldwide.

The legend is Ruth added the chocolate to the cookie batter by mistake. She was asked the truth of that tale on many occasions and simply answered that question with a wink and a smile. Ruth died in 1977 and took that secret with her. My guess is that accident or not, no one is upset about the delicious result.

THE MUTE SWANS OF SOUTHERN NEW HAMPSHIRE

In the marshy bog on Route 1 across the road from Jenness Beach in Rye New Hampshire, there is a small clutch of about six mute swans.

For centuries, the English regarded swans as a food. Nicks on bills or feet indicated a farmer's ownership. They were considered to be an all-purpose type of creature. The feathers were used in pillows or fashioned into quills for writing. Their bones could be carved into whistles and their webbed feet sewn together to make ladies' purses . . . not exactly the desired fate for the star of The Ugly Duckling.

The Swan Boats in Boston came to Boston in 1877. They became an instant hit and the subject of at least two popular children's books.

The swans themselves were released into Boston Public Gardens in 1909. Between 1910 and 1912, the swans were introduced to the lower Hudson Valley and Long Island. It is now estimated that there are approximately 4,000 such birds in southern coastal New England. The northernmost region to have such birds is the tip of southern Maine.

In the marshy bog on Route 1 across the road from Jenness Beach in Rye New Hampshire, there us a small clutch of about six mute swans. Since the birds rarely nest in colonies, it must be assumed that it is a family unit – an adult male (a cob), and adult female (a pen), and the nearly-grown young cygrets. Thus, the swans here are a beautiful rarity to the region. They are year-round residents, so they won't disappear during the winter months (unless, of course, you can't see them in the snow).

In the case of the swans of southern New Hampshire, the people flock to them. It is common to see several cars pull to the side of the road to allow travelers to watch and photograph these spectacular birds. Frankly, they come so close to the shoreline that they appear to be posing for the best shots. Shyness does not seem to be one of their major characteristics.

They are magnificent to behold. They are about five feet in length with a six-foot wingspan. They are completely covered in snowy white feathers and have a long, gracefully curved neck and a bright orange bill. In flight, they produce a deep, whirring sound.

Contrary to popular belief, mute swans do cheat on their spouses. They even take another mate if the original dies. It has been reported that this may happen before the feathers are cold on the deceased.

Treat yourself and your family. Take a drive up Route 1. Pull to the side of the road near the bog at Jenness Beach. The mute swans will quietly welcome you.

SOME MYTHS OF NEW ENGLAND

The sightings were so numerous, that a member of George Washington's staff compiled a report of them and published it in the Linnean Society of New England.

Most myths have at least a toehold in reality. Somebody sees young girls dancing and singing in a room as they sweep a floor. A few cats rush out the door in fright. Almost immediately, we have to deal with a witch problem . . . right here in Salem city!

Well, aside from UFOs, Champie and a coven of teenage witches, some rural New England residents have seen some frightening things going bump in the night, sometimes in the daytime, too!

The Dover Demon (That's Massachusetts, not New Hampshire) was first sighted in April 1977 at a stone wall. He was hairless with a baby's body and had bulging eyes and long spindly limbs. Sounds to me as though Gollum was out for a stroll.

Sightings of Bigfoot go back more than a century. The Algonquin tribes knew him as Windigo. For the most part, he seems to be traipsing about in the Berkshires. He probably just can't get enough of that great music at Tanglewood.

For over 200 years, folks around Cape Ann and Gloucester have had more than a few encounters with an 80-100 foot long critter called Casco Bay Sea Serpent. The sightings were so numerous, that a member of George Washington's staff compiled a report of them and published it in the Linnean Society of New England. Of late, however, it seems that this Cassie, complete with horns, hump and turtle's head may have moved to the region around Mount Desert Island, Maine. I think he or she just got tired of all the attention by the press.

There may be something in the skies over Easton, Massachusetts. Folks around Bird Hill report a creature with a wingspan of 8-12 feet perched at the edge of the Hockomock Swamp. The "Birdman" or the "Thunderbird" has also been reported to have been flying over various intersections. It could be that this fellow just can't work his GPS and wants to get back to Arizona.

Cape Cod may attract more than just tourists. In 1981, the "Beast of Truro" began killing pets and livestock. It was reported to weigh over 80 pounds and had a long, "ropelike" tail. In January 1982, two pigs were mauled to death in their pens. Since then, the attacks have ceased. Say, wasn't that about the time that the vegan movement kicked into high gear?

There may have been a giant frog in the Silver Lake region of Massachusetts's Plymouth County. Known as the "Frogman," this creature would pop up every now and again during the 1940's and '50's. This has nothing to do with the alligator sightings in the Saugus area some fifty years later. C'mon, frogs don't look anything like alligators!

From northern Maine to southeastern Massachusetts, from the 1930s to present day, folks continue to report sightings of a giant white bull moose. This Bullwinkle is supposed to be enormous, with antlers over ten feet in length, weighing over 2,500 pounds and standing about 15 feet tall. Those sighting the Spectre Moose are asked to call Hollywood; Rocky misses him greatly.

The Bridgewater Triangle in Massachusetts (not to be confused with the Bermuda Triangle) has had more than its share of bizarre creature sightings. Native Americans in the area report stories of the Pukwudgees, or "little man of the forest." You'll know him if you see him. He has gray skin, large ears, fingers and nose. He can shape shift and start fires magically. He may be found in the vicinity of some large boa constrictors. Makes you want to pack a picnic basket, grab the kids and head off to the country, doesn't it?

DOING YOUR HEART
A WORLD OF GOOD

Go for a walk around Federal Hill in Providence, Rhode Island.

If you want to do your heart a world of good, go for a walk. If you want to do your heart a world of good, and put a smile on your face, go for a walk around Federal Hill in Providence, Rhode Island.

The area is known as "The Heartbeat of Providence." It begins under the pineapple arch at Atwells Avenue. Even if you're not Italian, you will feel as though you've just gone home to be welcomed into the loving arms of your family. Everything about the locale brings smiles to the faces of those who slowly make the pilgrimage from Atwells Avenue to Broadway, and from Westminster Street to Cranston Street.

"The Hill" is the Little Italy you always wanted to experience, even if you didn't know you wanted to experience it. It is a true sensual delight. You would be hard-pressed to walk only a few feet without hearing an animated conversation in Italian. Then again, you don't have to strain your ears to hear Chinese, Lebanese, Spanish, or Middle Eastern conversations as well.

The colors of the buildings are vibrant and truly lend themselves to gaity and wonderful experiences to be shared or not. . . It's your choice. Speaking of color, you will be dazzled by the array of foods in the various eateries. From Angelo's to Joe Mazilli's Old Canteen, the décor and the foods are sensual delights to write home about.

Now, I know a trip to the market doesn't usually sound like an occasion to remember, but my guess is that you've never shopped at the Venda Vavioli or at Scialo's Bakery. Mama mia! My stomach has a memory, and it's telling me that it's time for another road trip to Federal Hill.

You want a little more local flavor? Go to any of a number of cafes and enjoy a cup of espresso or cappuccino out of doors while you listen to a recording of a Sicilian mandolin or a vintage Frank Sinatra album wafting from the topmost floor of a nearby three-decker. Ah, what an experience!

Without a doubt, every day is a festival of joy in the Heartbeat of Providence, but if you want just a bit more pizzazz, you'll have to experience the Columbus Day Weekend Festival. This three-day Italian event has been recognized as one of the best Columbus Day events in the country! The food and entertainment is second to none.

Okay, enough said. Go for a walk.

THE RUSSO/JAPAN TREATY

*Moreover, it was President Theodore Roosevelt who was
key in helping to facilitate the Treaty. For his efforts,
Roosevelt earned the Nobel Peace Prize.*

Through the years, the Portsmouth Naval Shipyard in Kittery Maine has
been the scene of major events in this country's history. The Ranger, commanded by Captain John Paul Jones was commissioned there. Prisoners
from the Spanish-American War in 1898 were housed there. And, through
the years, numerous warships, including an amazing host of submarines
were launched or repaired at this location. In May of 1945, the German
U-Boat U-234 was captured on the high seas and towed into the Portsmouth
Naval Yard. It was reported that it was transporting a load of uranium to an
undisclosed South American country at the time. Indeed, the shipyard holds
one other distinction.

On September 5, 1905, the Treaty of Portsmouth was signed. This treaty
formally ended the Russo-Japanese War. Moreover, it was President Theodore Roosevelt who was key in helping to facilitate the Treaty. For his efforts,
Roosevelt earned the Nobel Peace Prize.

The bloody war, 1904-05, featured Russia with one of the largest armies in
the world driving south into Manchuria intent on seizing Japan's industrial
region. In the process, however, Russia suffered severe naval losses. The out-
come was a very real threat of revolution against the Russian government.

After a series of Japanese military victories, Japan believed that the time
was right to move toward a settlement. The Japanese Army Minister, Ter-
auchi Masatake conveyed to Roosevelt that Japan was ready to negotiate.

Roosevelt strongly suggested a neutral location, that being Kittery, Maine.
Twelve meetings were held in the General Store Building, with furniture ordered from Washington.

Japan was adamant about reparations being made by Russia but realized
there was little hope in achieving this goal. Ultimately, Japan settled upon
taking ownership of the southern half of the Sakhalin.

The Treaty of Portsmouth was signed on September 5, 1905.

In 1994, the Portsmouth Peace Treaty Forum was formed by the Japanese-
American Society of New Hampshire. This forum brought to light one of the
greatest symbols of peace in the North Pacific region.

AMERICAN'S STONEHENGE
AN ANCIENT MYSTERY

Who crafted these stones into this structure
remains a mystery.

Some believe it to be 4,000 years old. Some say it is dates back ten millennia. Some think it is merely a fake. Whatever the truth, American's Stonehenge, located in Salem, New Hampshire still attracts crowds from near and far who attempt to sleuth their way to the truth.

Located near Mystery Hill is a maze of stone chambers created by large standing stones. The stones were apparently astronomically oriented to be aligned with the summer solstice, winter solstice, mid summer solstice and the mid-winter solstice.

Who crafted these stones into this structure remains a mystery. Some believe it was an ancient culture not widely known in North America. Others believe it to be the work of the Celts, Norsemen or other European peoples. Whoever created this stone oddity also left behind a sacrificial table, so chances are good that the location was not designed as a summer camp.

Another amazing curiosity about the Salem Stonehenge is that if one were to line a laser shot across the Atlantic Ocean at the "front door" of Stonehenge in England, it would zip in perfectly. My guess is that even with today's precision technology, accomplishing that feat would not be such an easy chore.

The stones, some weighing over four tons were groove-scored, so they would fit together perfectly and drain effectively. Scholars continue to debate just who may have had the technological savvy, physical means and time to produce a complex of this magnitude. Even the ancient fire pit and pottery fragments found at the site offer no clues.

Having traipsed the area on several occasions, I could almost swear I heard ancient voices chanting some dark ritual to a solemn and dark drumbeat. Then again, it could have been simply the breeze blowing lightly through the maple trees.

Is it worth a visit? Truly, yes . . . but bring your own answers. Nobody else seems to have any.

CADILLAC MOUNTAIN

It is the first place in the United States to view the sunrise.

No, it's not the tallest of all mountains, but Cadillac Mountain in Acadia National Park in Maine holds one amazing distinction. It is the first place in the United States to view the sunrise. That fact may not be earth-shattering, but if you're standing there as the sun creeps over the eastern horizon, your feeling is that this commonplace spectacle is simply extraordinarily beautiful!

Okay, backtracking just a little . . . the distinction of being the first place in the country only occurs during the spring and summer. Mars Hill, located just a little to the northeast holds first place the rest of the time.

Witnessing sunrise there is truly a photo op. The colors on the horizon are brilliant in their majesty. You'll definitely want to make sure you have plenty of battery power for all of the shots you'll be taking.

According to Arcadia blog, there are five things you definitely should to make sure you enjoy your sunrise experience:

1. Make sure you give yourself time to get to the top. It's about a 20-minute drive from the village to Bar Harbor. If you are late, there are no re-dos.

2. Dress warmly. You certainly don't want to shiver when you're snapping a photograph. Wind and chill up there are definite considerations.

3. Bring a blanket and chairs. Your wait won't be long, but you do want to be comfortable.

4. If you are a coffee-drinker, bring a full thermos.   If you   don't drink coffee, hot chocolate will suffice.

5. Get your camera angle ready. The colors at sunrise won't last very long. Within less than a minute, the morning sky will wash out the glory of that magic moment. Be ready!

Oh, for the record, the mountain was not named after a car. It was named so to honor French explorer and adventurer, Antoine Laument de La Mothe, sieur de Cadillac. For all the work he had done charting the region, De la Mothe requested a parcel of land in the area known as Donaquec. In 1688, he received the land, and thereafter it became known as sieur de Cadillac.

There are several hiking trails to the mountain's summit. There is also a paved road if you don't want to stumble before the sun rises. On a clear day, one may see Mount Katahdin, Maine's highest mountain as well as the Canadian province of Nova Scotia, both over one hundred miles away.

Take the trip. Have some coffee. Frame the pics. Give my regards to the sunrise.

CHRISTMAS IN HAMPTON

T'was Christmas in Hampton
With snow and with lights.
The chill in the air
Made the season so right.

The shops in the town
Had presents a glimmer.
The ice on the ponds
Was pure crystal and silver.

Churches had candles
And each had a manger.
All were so welcome,
There was nary a stranger.

Aromas from kitchens
Were rich and delicious.
The food was aplenty,
And filled all the dishes.

And down by the seacoast
The folks were all cheery.
The taverns were open
The atmosphere merry.

The children sang carols,
Or took part in plays.
They waited for Santa,
Just counting the days.

All around Route 1
T'was wreaths and t'was holly.
The lovers brought presents,
And shopped to share coffee.

Yes, t'was Christmas in Hampton.
With trees to adorn.
T'was Christmas in Hampton,
Who could ask for much more?

THE RAKE

Autumn really is a glorious season in wondrous New England. As summer wanes, the first maple leaves begin to yellow. They go virtually unnoticed by many, except for the truly seasoned. We watch, sigh and begin to prepare for that leaf and all of his friends to cascade in torrents into our yards.

I recall one of the very first creative writing assignments from the fourth grade. The topic was fall, and the first line of my little essay went, "Did you ever stand on a Sunday in fall and watch the gaily-colored leaves float on a gentle breeze to the ground?" I was very naïve. I had yet to go mano-a-mano with The Leaf Army.

In junior high school, I did all sorts of odd jobs to put some coins in my pocket. One job was raking leaves. So, I bought my own rake. I found it to be an extremely easy tool to care for, requiring virtually no maintenance. One straightens out any crooked tines, hangs it in the shed and it is good to go again next year, and the next, ad infinitum.

I still have that rake. I had planned to bequeath it to one of my three sons-- two now live in Las Vegas and one is in the oil fields of Texas. None of my sons have ever held a rake, nor have they expressed any desire to do so.

From a Zen prospective, I am "one with my rake." Most of my neighbors utilize 21st century technology for the annual Great Leaf Roundup. They have riding lawnmowers with mulchers and giant attached receptacles or portable, three-speed leaf blower backpacks with tent-like structures for trapping. Me, I have my handy rake and the same masonry trash bags I bought ten years ago. (My previous batch wore out.)

I wear an old t-shirt when I rake. On the front is my own personal slogan, "WHO NEEDS A GYM? I HAVE A RAKE!"

I read that Agatha Christie got inspirations for her murder mysteries while doing dishes. I get mine while raking leaves. I'm not sure if my neighbors have inspirations while waving their leaf blowers.

The trees are bare now. I've straightened the tines on my rake and hung it in the shed. I bought a fat cigar and smoked it while I sat on my stone wall, surveying my leaf-free lawn. Story lines play tag among my brain cells. I'll probably go inside and jot them down. But first, I have one more chore.

I must bring out my snow shovel and prop it next to the porch.